YORK NOTES

General Editors: Professor A.N. Jeffares (*University of Stirling*) & Professor Suheil Bushrui (*American University of Beirut*)

John Steinbeck

THE PEARL

Notes by Margaret Yong

BA (SINGAPORE) MA (MALAYA)
Lecturer in English, University of Malaya

**LONGMAN
YORK PRESS**

YORK PRESS
Immeuble Esseily, Place Riad Solh, Beirut.

LONGMAN GROUP LIMITED
Longman House, Burnt Mill, Harlow,
Essex CM20 2JE, England
and Associated Companies throughout the world

First published 1981, reprinted 1983 and 1985
ISBN 0 582 78127 2
Produced by Longman Group (FE) Ltd
Printed in Hong Kong

Contents

Part 1: Introduction *page* 5
  General introduction 5
  Background to *The Pearl* 11
  A note on the text 13

Part 2: Summaries 15
  A general summary 15
  Detailed summaries 17

Part 3: Commentary 35
  The nature of *The Pearl* 35
  The Pearl as a social document 36
  The characters 40
  The ideas 47
  Style and meaning 54
  The theme 63

Part 4: Hints for study 65
  The plot 65
  Characterisation 66
  The setting 68
  The style 69
  The arrangement of material 70
  Useful quotations 74
  Context questions 79
  Interpretative questions 81
  Model answers 81

Part 5: Suggestions for further reading 85

The author of these notes 87

Part 1

Introduction

General introduction

John Ernst Steinbeck was born on 27 February 1902 in Salinas, California. The country where he grew up is a fertile green valley, bounded by the Gabilan and Santa Lucia Mountains and by the sea. This region deeply affected Steinbeck and provided the background for many of his novels: the world of his childhood is evoked sensitively in *The Red Pony* (1933). Steinbeck came from a middle-class family. His father operated a flour mill and for many years was the treasurer of Monterey County. His mother, Olive Hamilton, a school-teacher, was portrayed by Steinbeck in *East of Eden* (1952). She encouraged Steinbeck to read and he was acquainted as a child with the works of Flaubert, Dostoevsky, Milton, Hardy and George Eliot. However, the books that influenced him most were the King James version of the Bible and Malory's *Morte d'Arthur*.

Steinbeck went to Salinas High School and Stanford University, where he studied literature and marine biology, although without taking a degree. During this time he held a series of temporary jobs, including working as a ranch hand, an assistant chemist in a sugar refinery, a labourer in a road building gang and a fisherman in Monterey. After leaving Stanford, he lived briefly in New York, where he worked on a newspaper and also as a labourer helping to build Madison Square Garden. His close and varied experience with a variety of people can be felt in the freshness and sympathy with which he describes the life of the community in his early novels.

His first novel, *Cup of Gold* (1929), was not characteristic of Steinbeck's well-known novels. It was about Henry Morgan, the seventeenth-century buccaneer. With his next two novels, Steinbeck discovered his true subject. The familiar central California scene of his early life forms the setting of *The Pastures of Heaven* (1932) and *To a God Unknown* (1933). Henceforth, his best fiction was concerned with California, the true source of his inspiration.

In 1930 Steinbeck married Carol Henning and they lived in Pacific Grove near Monterey. He was still a struggling, unknown writer and they were very poor, needing the twenty-five dollars a month subsidy given to them by Steinbeck's father, who wanted his son to concentrate on his writing career.

With his next novel, *Tortilla Flat* (1935), Steinbeck at last achieved a degree of fame and success. *Tortilla Flat* was a best-seller, which won the California Commonwealth Club gold medal for the year's best novel by a California writer. It brought financial independence to Steinbeck for the first time. He visited Mexico, a country that always fascinated him, but found he could not write there and returned to Los Gatos, California.

Tortilla Flat presented an ironic, humorous, yet affectionate portrayal of the very poor drifters of Monterey, during the economic Depression of the 1930s. Below its witty surface, the novel had an allegorical meaning based on the legend of King Arthur and his Knights of the Round Table.

Tortilla Flat was the first of a series of novels on which Steinbeck's literary reputation rests. While seeming to cover a disparate range of materials, these major works are unified by a characteristic vision of existence. In all Steinbeck's early fiction may be felt the shaping pressure of his 'biological', or 'non-teleological', view of life. This was essentially a way of looking at things that Steinbeck developed in close association with Edward Ricketts.

Steinbeck met Ricketts in a dentist's waiting room in Monterey, and they quickly became friends. Ricketts owned Pacific Biological Laboratories on Cannery Row in Monterey and Steinbeck often joined him in searching for marine organisms in the tidal basins of Monterey Bay for this laboratory. Ricketts became the model for some central figures in Steinbeck's fiction: Doc Burton in *In Dubious Battle*, Doc in *Cannery Row* and *Sweet Thursday* and the hero of a short story, 'The Snake'. After Ricketts's death, Steinbeck wrote a personal tribute, which was published as 'About Ed Ricketts'.

Steinbeck and Ricketts shared the view that life could best be understood by accepting the fact that life simply 'is', and that it should not be 'explained' by reference to man-made philosophical structures. Steinbeck termed this way of thinking 'is-thinking'. This view has been called a 'biological view' of life by critics, since it rests on the assumption that human existence closely parallels biological life, such as that found in the tide pool, and that the processes of life, death, and procreation are all part of an organic whole.

The biological view of life is put forward in *Sea of Cortez* (1941), the journal of an expedition to the Gulf of California (which used to be known as the Sea of Cortez) which Steinbeck and Ricketts made in March–April 1940. *Sea of Cortez* consisted of two parts, firstly the scientific record of the collection of marine animals in the littoral, and secondly the philosophical portion in which the daily log of their movements and discussions was kept. Later, Steinbeck published the philosophical part separately as *The Log from the Sea of Cortez* (1951).

During the middle years of the 1930s, Steinbeck became increasingly concerned with social developments in California itself. He documented this period of history in *In Dubious Battle* (1936), 'The Harvest Gypsies', a series of articles for the San Francisco *Chronicle* (5–12 October 1936), and *The Grapes of Wrath* (1939), which was tentatively called *L'Affaire Lettuceburg*. The sociological material of *In Dubious Battle* and *The Grapes of Wrath* was typical of the realistic 'proletarian' writing of this era.

The title of *In Dubious Battle* is a phrase from Milton's *Paradise Lost*, which suggests the uneasy and ambiguous nature of man's struggle to improve the conditions of his existence. *In Dubious Battle* depicts the plight of the migrant workers in California's farms and orchards.

This theme was developed in *The Grapes of Wrath* (1939), Steinbeck's most famous novel, which won the Pulitzer Prize in 1940 for the best novel of the preceding year and which was made into an important social protest film later. The background for *The Grapes of Wrath* was the trek to California on an epic scale by the tenant farmers of the American south-west. The farmers had been forced by prolonged drought to leave this area where over-farming had turned the once rich prairie soil into a virtual desert, known as the 'Dust Bowl', and they faced grave problems of social dislocation.

An earlier novel, *Of Mice and Men* (1937), had also dealt with migrant workers in a California ranch background. But the story is concerned with the relationship between two ranch hands, rather than with the larger, overt, sociological implications of the community.

Steinbeck had made the expedition to the Gulf of California in 1940 partly to escape the insanity of the Second World War. He could not ignore it, though, in his work. In fact, he wrote a promotional book, *Bombs Away* (1942), for the Air Force. His other war contributions included *The Moon is Down* (1942), *Lifeboat*, a film scenario, and *Once There Was a War*, a collection of articles written as a war correspondent for the New York *Herald Tribune*, which was published in 1958.

In 1942 Steinbeck and Carol Henning were divorced and a year later, in March 1943, he married his second wife, Gwen Verdon. She gave him two sons, Tom and John, Steinbeck's only children, who were depicted in *East of Eden*. This marriage also ended in divorce (1948) and in December 1950 Steinbeck married his third wife, Elaine Scott. By this time, Steinbeck had left California permanently and settled in New York. He only visited California irregularly, but the region of his developing years continued to exert an influence upon his work.

Steinbeck continued to pay tribute to his native state in his fiction, producing *Cannery Row* (1945), *The Wayward Bus* (1947), *East of Eden* (1952) and *Sweet Thursday* (1954), which all use California as their background. Steinbeck's post-war novels have been considered as a return to the early sentimentality of his works. Critical opinion has been harsh on Steinbeck's writing after the Second World War. But critical estimation of *Cannery Row*, at least, has tended to place a higher valuation on this novel as a serious attempt by Steinbeck to formulate his non-teleological vision of life.

Cannery Row is based on the view, implicit in all Steinbeck's major works, that life forms a harmonious and well-ordered whole. With gently probing irony, the novel deals with the mutually gratifying and supporting relationship between the philosopher-scientist hero, Doc, and the outcasts and loafers of the Row.

The novel has been described as a 'poisoned cream-puff', a view which implies that beneath the superficial similarities with the humour of *Tortilla Flat* (which also dealt with social outcasts), *Cannery Row*, too, had a deeply satirical meaning.

Shortly after completing *Cannery Row*, Steinbeck began work on *The Pearl* (1947), based on a story he had heard on the expedition to the Gulf of California (Sea of Cortez) in 1940.

Cannery Row, *The Pearl* and *The Wayward Bus* can be regarded as an informal trilogy on different aspects of twentieth-century civilisation. *Cannery Row* scrutinises the hidden subculture formed by the social derelicts from a materially rich American society; *The Pearl*, although not set in America, offers a view of the corrupting influence of materialism on the spiritual quality of life; while *The Wayward Bus* can be considered as an examination of what happens when ordinary Americans are removed from the supporting props of normal society and are thrust into a hostile natural environment to fend for themselves.

The Wayward Bus makes use of a bus journey to initiate the action: a bus-load of representative types of Americans are stranded when their bus is driven off the highway by a heavy storm. The representative group is a symbolic motif of which Steinbeck had made use before, in *The Pastures of Heaven*, where a coach-full of tourists gaze into the beautiful valley of the pastures of heaven, and weave their dreams about a new life. The tourists are unaware that life in the paradisial valley is as full of a mixture of good and evil as the outside world.

In *The Pearl*, Steinbeck modified the basic idea of a representative group of human beings, who are transformed by the discovery of a flawless thing of beauty. *The Pearl*, like the symbolic valley of the heavenly pastures, arouses dreams of a fresh beginning in all who gaze upon it, but these dreams turn into avaricious greed and cruelty.

The theme of a fresh beginning was used frequently by Steinbeck. Because of its simplicity, this idea can suggest very basic motivations in human existence. It is a theme that is characteristic of American literature, for it points to a fundamental aspect of the concept of America as the 'New World', that is, a world of fresh possibilities in human life. In using this traditional theme in *The Pearl*, Steinbeck adds an unspoken dimension of meaning to his novel.

During the post-war years, Steinbeck immersed himself in his career. He was becoming increasingly a public personality, something which he had always feared would threaten his creativity as a writer. His critics, too, asserted that Steinbeck had failed his artistic vision and had not fulfilled the promise of his earlier books. *The Wayward Bus* brought him greater popularity with readers. It was chosen as a Book-of-the-Month Club selection, but the critics attacked its tendency to philosophise. Steinbeck began to feel that he was losing his literary energy. However, in 1948, he was elected to the American Academy of Arts.

During this period, too, he had gone through an unhappy personal life: he had divorced his second wife and had lost his best friend and mentor, Ed Ricketts, who was killed in an accident when his car was struck by a train near Monterey.

Perhaps to overcome his sense of loneliness and frustration, he involved himself in many projects, which, unfortunately, did not seem conducive to the writing of fiction. He visited Russia with the famous photographer, Robert Capa. The trip was financed by the New York *Herald Tribune*, and the primary aim was to discover how ordinary Russians were living after the destruction of the War. The result of this collaboration was produced in *A Russian Journal* (1948). Steinbeck also wrote film scripts for Hollywood, including the scripts for the film versions of *The Pearl* (1948) and *The Red Pony* (1949). Steinbeck wrote the screenplay for two films about Mexico, *The Forgotten Village* (1941), about the introduction of modern medicine to a primitive Mexican village, and *Viva Zapata!* (1952), based on the life of the Mexican revolutionary. In all, Steinbeck wrote or adapted for the screen thirteen stories, and narrated one film based on some short stories by the writer O. Henry. The most famous of Steinbeck's films are probably *The Grapes of Wrath* (1940) and *East of Eden* (1955), based on his own novels.

Steinbeck was interested in experimenting with the form of the novel. He had written *Of Mice and Men* and *The Moon is Down* (1942) as play-novellas, that is, novels in the form of a stage play, and they had been successfully staged. He now produced his third play-novella, *Burning Bright* (1959), but it failed almost immediately on Broadway and Steinbeck was very disheartened.

In December 1950 Steinbeck married Elaine Scott, his third wife. He continued to write fiction as well as film scripts and articles for magazines, but had produced no major work since *Cannery Row* and *The Pearl*. He had been thinking about a large writing project for three or four years, and in 1953 he began work on the novel which took him two years to complete. *East of Eden* constituted an emotional return to California. It was Steinbeck's attempt to explore his family's roots in the Salinas Valley and he was writing it in part for his two sons. He seemed to be entering a new phase in his life and career.

Steinbeck explained in *Journal of a Novel: The East of Eden Letters* (1969) that he had been revealing only the darker aspects of American life in his early works. He wanted to explore the more positive qualities of that civilisation, and *East of Eden* would be a major testament of his faith in America, for Steinbeck saw the novel as the culminating achievement of his literary career.

East of Eden was made into a successful film, but the novel never acquired the stature that Steinbeck hoped for it. The autobiographical parts dealing with his mother's family, the Hamiltons, often recalled the power and freshness of his early works, and the natural description of the landscape evoked Steinbeck's original source of strength. On the whole, though, the novel was cumbersome and flat. The central story about the Trask family was stiff and unreal.

After *East of Eden* Steinbeck's writing declined in quality. In the 1950s appeared *Sweet Thursday*, a sentimental sequel to *Cannery Row*, and *The Short Happy Reign of Pippin IV* (1957); and there were some short stories and magazine articles which could not be taken seriously.

During the decade of the 1960s, Steinbeck wrote only one novel, *The Winter of Our Discontent* (1960), and two documentaries: *Travels with Charley in Search of America* (1962), an account of an overland journey he made between Maine on the Atlantic coast and California, with just his dog, Charley, for company; and *America and Americans* (1967) which is largely a photographic record of America.

The Winter of Our Discontent owes its title to Shakespeare's *Richard III* and its style is influenced by the Bible and T.S. Eliot's *The Waste Land*. These influences reinforce the theme, which is a satirical record of the moral failure of modern, affluent American society. The action is set in Sag Harbour, Long Island, where Steinbeck was living. Steinbeck had lived in New York briefly in 1925 and since 1943 he had decided to make it his more or less permanent place of residence. However, his fictional work continued to rely on California for its theme and background, and *The Winter of Our Discontent* is his only important work to be set outside that region.

In 1962 Steinbeck was awarded the Nobel Prize for Literature. Winning the highest literary honour seemed to sap his creative energy, for he never wrote any significant fiction after that. Perhaps, as he had always feared, success and fame made him self-conscious as a writer.

Steinbeck's achievement has been questioned by hostile critics, who feel that the initial potential of his novels was never developed. Steinbeck's accomplishment is a substantial one, though, for he has produced a great variety of works, including novels, short stories, plays, and film scripts. Moreover, he has written great works like *The Grapes of Wrath*, *Tortilla Flat* and *Cannery Row*.

Steinbeck died on 20 December 1968 at his apartment in New York City, and is buried in Salinas, California, where he was born.

Background to *The Pearl*

The Pearl was written in the winter of 1944–5, before the newly published *Cannery Row* appeared in the bookshops. The basic idea for the novella (a technical name for a short novel—see page 13) came from an ostensibly true story that Steinbeck heard on his scientific expedition to the Gulf of California in 1940.

On this trip, Steinbeck visited the ancient city of La Paz, situated on the southern end of Baja (Lower) California, which was a narrow peninsula of land separated from mainland Mexico by the Gulf of California. La Paz had once been a great pearl trading centre. Baja California was still a remote and primitive region, a harsh land of snow-covered mountains and arid steep valleys with some subsistence farming where water could be obtained from wells. In this region, Mexicans of native Indian origin lived in isolated communities, on the fringes of larger towns, often in conditions of extreme poverty. Mexicans descended from the Spanish conquistadores, or conquerors of Mexico, generally lived in the wealthier sections of town.

After four hundred years, this ethnic polarisation could still be felt in Kino's community. In *The Pearl* there is a keen sense of racial antagonism between the poor Indian pearl divers and fishermen and the Spanish-Mexican professional classes, like the doctor and priest.

At La Paz, Steinbeck picked up a story that was widely known as a folk-tale in Baja California. He recounted this tale in *Sea of Cortez* in fewer than 350 words.

An Indian boy by accident found a pearl of great size, an unbelievable pearl. He knew its value was so great that he need never work again. In his one pearl he had the ability to be drunk as long as he wished, to marry any one of a number of girls, and to make many more a little happy too. In his great pearl lay salvation, for he could in advance purchase masses sufficient to pop him out of Purgatory like a squeezed water-melon seed. In addition he could shift a number of dead relatives a little nearer to Paradise. He went to La Paz with his pearl in his hand and his future clear into eternity in his heart. He took his pearl to a broker and was offered so little that he grew angry, for he knew he was cheated. Then he carried his pearl to another broker and was offered the same amount. After a few more visits he came to know that the brokers were only the many hands of one head and that he could not sell his pearl for more. He took it to the beach and hid it under a stone, and that night he was clubbed into unconsciousness and his clothing was searched. The next night he slept at the house of a friend and his friend and he were injured and bound and the whole house searched. Then he went inland to lose his pursuers and he was waylaid and tortured. But he was very angry and he knew what he must do. Hurt as he was he crept back to La Paz in the night and he skulked like a hunted fox to the beach and took out his pearl from under the stone. Then he cursed it and threw it as far as he could into the channel. He was a free man again with his soul in danger and his food and shelter insecure. And he laughed a great deal about it.

Steinbeck nursed the story in his mind for four years before using it in his own version of the tale of the pearl. He felt that the original story did not sound believable, because it seemed so much like a parable, or a short story with a hidden moral lesson. He was particularly dissatisfied with the figure of the Indian boy who found the pearl. The boy seemed to Steinbeck to be 'too heroic, too wise . . . he goes contrary to human direction.'*

Steinbeck greatly expanded the simple story of the pearl, in order to emphasise certain aspects of the folk-tale. The main effect of the transformation was to humanise the characters in the story and to add significantly to the spiritual and emotional content in the story.

The principal change that Steinbeck made was to convert the heroic figure of the boy to a mature young man with a wife and baby. In doing so, he immediately enlarged the human significance of the story, for the man, woman, and child become representative of the whole family of man.

Steinbeck also developed the social context of the story. The life of the community is depicted in some detail. Steinbeck explores the relationships between the Indian fishermen and pearl divers and the more sophisticated town dwellers, who are contemptuous of their poorer neighbours.

The novel may also have been influenced by two other sources. The first of these is the story of the man who sells all he has in order to buy a pearl of great value, which is recorded in the Bible (Matthew 13:45-6). The second source is 'The Hymn of the Soul', sometimes called 'The Hymn of the Pearl'.† This hymn is a poem sung by the apostle, St Thomas, in prison. It tells of the journey of an eastern prince to Egypt,

*John Steinbeck, *Sea of Cortez*, Viking Press, New York, 1941, pp.102–3.
† 'The Hymn of the Pearl' is preserved in the Acts of Thomas, which date from the third century. The Acts of Thomas reflect the teachings of gnosticism, a philosophical movement which deviated from the doctrine of the early Christian Church. As such, the Acts of Thomas are apocryphal, not being an accepted part of the Protestant Bible.

on a mission to find the pearl. Being waylaid, he forgets his mission and almost loses his soul, but finally accomplishes his task and secures his soul.

In Steinbeck's version, Kino also gives up everything and goes on a desert journey, for the sake of the pearl, which he calls 'my soul'. The pearl becomes evil, however, and he only saves his soul by throwing the pearl back into the sea.

The Pearl is written in the form of a novella, that is, a prose narrative longer than a short story but shorter than a novel. It has been called a play-novella, a literary form that particularly interested Steinbeck. He had written *Of Mice and Men* as a play-novella which had been staged very successfully on Broadway. He saw the hybrid form of the play-novella as a novel written in the form of a play (or a play in the form of a novel), and making use of direct dramatic action, presented very tightly and with little authorial intrusion to comment on the meaning.

The Pearl contains a number of dramatic elements, such as the direct revelation of character through action and dialogue. It also has a symphonic or musical quality, derived from the use of songs as motifs that carry the theme, and are repeated or modified as the story develops. On the other hand, *The Pearl* is not like a play, because the author follows an old tradition of the novel in being omniscient, or able to comment on the significance of the action from a superior or detached vantage point.

At the time that Steinbeck wrote *The Pearl*, he was curious about film techniques because many of his own novels were made into films during the 1940s. *The Pearl* was produced as a film using Mexican actors and a Mexican director. Inevitably, *The Pearl* reflects Steinbeck's interest in cinematic techniques. Its visual impact and sense of rhythmic continuity are very strong features of its style. The visual beauty of *The Pearl* was captured effectively in the opening scenes of the film version, as the camera composed Steinbeck's description of the distant mountains, the curve of the shoreline, and the robed women and white-clad men.

The Pearl, in its film version, can be seen in the context of Steinbeck's other films of Mexico, *The Forgotten Village* and *Viva Zapata!* These films bring out Steinbeck's concern for the underprivileged in a society that exploits the poor. Mexican peasant life, as *The Pearl* clearly suggests, can be brutal and fatalistic.

A note on the text

The Pearl first appeared under the title 'The Pearl of the World' in *Woman's Home Companion* in December 1945. With its title shortened to *The Pearl*, the book version was published by Viking Press in 1947 to coincide with the release of the film based on it.

Editions in print today include those published by Viking Press

(1965), Pan Books (1970), and Penguin (1976), all in paperback; Heinemann Educational Books (New Windmill Series, 1977), an illustrated edition; and it is also available in the Heinemann Guided Readers Series (1974).

Page references to *The Pearl* throughout these Notes are to the edition in 'The New Windmill Series' published by William Heinemann, London, 1977.

Part 2

Summaries
of THE PEARL

A general summary

Kino, a poor fisherman, lives peacefully with his wife Juana and their baby son Coyotito in a brush house on the beach near La Paz. The harmony of their world is shattered one lovely morning, when the enemy* in the form of a scorpion stings Coyotito; Kino hears the Song of the Enemy.† Juana sucks the poison from the puncture, but, frightened for the baby's life, insists on seeing the doctor. They proceed to town, followed by all their neighbours. The doctor, who is an ignorant, cruel, and greedy man, instructs his servant to send them away after making sure that they have no money to pay for treatment. Kino, feeling bitterly humiliated, strikes his fist on the doctor's closed gate, drawing blood from his knuckles.

Kino returns to the beach with his family and they go out in their canoe, hoping to find a pearl valuable enough to pay for the doctor's treatment. Kino searches among the rocks of the sea bottom, to the inner accompaniment of the secret music of the Song of the Pearl That Might Be. He finds a very large oyster lying by itself, brings it to the canoe, opens it, and discovers the most beautiful and perfect pearl in the world. At the same moment, Juana discovers that Coyotito seems to be recovering from the scorpion sting.

The town hums with excitement at the news: the priest, the doctor, the beggars, the pearl buyers, consider enviously how such a valuable pearl might bring joy to their own lives. By some mysterious process, the possession of the pearl has made Kino every man's enemy. Unconscious of the evil growing around them, Kino and Juana plan happily for the future. They will be married in church and wear fine clothes; Kino will buy a harpoon and a rifle; and Coyotito will go to school. Drawn by the pearl, the priest comes to their brush house and Kino again hears the music of the enemy. Later the doctor arrives and pretends to examine the baby, who is now almost completely recovered.

*Steinbeck employs this term in a general way; here it applies to the scorpion, later to the priest.

†See notes on the songs, pp.55–7. These songs reflect Kino's inner state of mind, for instance, his sense of peace with the natural world in the morning, his sense of danger when the scorpion attacks or when the priest visits him. Sometimes Juana, too, seems to hear the songs, but it is not clear whether other people can hear this music.

Their fear awakened by the cunning doctor, Kino and Juana permit the doctor to treat Coyotito. When they are alone again, Kino buries the pearl in the dirt (earth) floor of their brush hut. During the night Kino is hurt when he fights with an intruder who comes into their hut to search for the pearl. Juana, frightened, begs Kino to destroy the pearl before it destroys them. Kino is determined that they shall have the bright future promised by the pearl. The beauty of the pearl lulls them into a false sense of security and they begin the second day with new hope.

Accompanied by neighbours and other town people, they go into La Paz to sell their pearl to the buyers, who really represent only one man. The first buyer is experienced in his dealings and contemptuously dismisses the pearl as a curiosity worth little. To demonstrate his good faith, he summons three other dealers, who are secretly his accomplices. They belittle the pearl and offer even less. Angrily, Kino refuses to sell the pearl, determined to get a better price even if he must go to the capital itself. Kino's brother, Juan Tomás, warns him that he has threatened the whole structure of life and will suffer the consequences of his defiance. Worried and depressed, Kino has become afraid even of the darkness around his home, but goes out to meet the unknown terrors of the night. After this second assault on Kino, Juana again pleads with him to destroy the pearl. Kino has made up his mind that they will sell the pearl in the capital city.

Early in the morning of the third day, Juana takes the pearl and runs to the beach. Kino awakens and prevents her from throwing the pearl back into the sea. He is enraged and strikes her, then, disgusted with himself, he walks up the beach towards his brush house. He is attacked once more, and, in the scuffle, kills his assailant. As he is now a murderer, they have no choice but to flee. Kino discovers that his precious canoe has been destroyed; at the same time, his brush house has been set on fire. The family takes refuge in Kino's brother's house until evening when they leave quietly for the north.

They walk all night and at dawn hide in a little clearing near the road. Kino takes out his pearl to look for the bright vision of the future. Instead he sees the dreadful images of the past few days: a dead body with blood dripping from its throat, the beaten Juana crawling on the ground, and Coyotito's feverish face. The music of the pearl has become evil to Kino. Kino sleeps uneasily and awakes to find that men from the town have discovered their trail. He sees three men in the distance, one on horseback and two on foot who are trackers. Kino wants to surrender, but Juana convinces him that the hunters would not spare any of their lives. They are now hunted like animals. They flee toward the mountains. Kino wants Juana to hide with the baby, while he draws the hunters away, but Juana will not leave him. Kino gains strength from

Juana's resolution and they press on, towards a little spring with pools of water in the mountains. They hide in a small cave, hoping the hunters will miss them. However, the hunters stop to rest by the pool, as night is approaching; two of the men sleep, while one watches, holding the rifle. Kino knows their only chance is to kill the men, before dawn reveals their hiding place. He formulates a plan and tells Juana that if he is killed, she must go on with the baby to Loreto in the north. His plan goes wrong. As the watching man fires from his rifle, Kino leaps on him and kills first him and then the other two men. Only then does he hear the hysterical cry of death from the cave.

Late in the afternoon of the fifth day, Kino and Juana return to La Paz. Juana is carrying the little heavy bundle of her dead child in her shawl, and Kino has a rifle across his arm. They seem to be walking in a strangely mesmerised state, as though unaware of their surroundings, so that people looking at them are overawed. Together they go down to the beach. Kino takes the pearl in his hand and gazes into it for the last time. To Kino the pearl looks ugly and its music is distorted; in it he sees little Coyotito with the top of his head shot away. Kino offers the pearl to Juana, who says softly, 'No, you.' He flings the pearl into the sea and it sinks down through the water. As the pearl vanishes, the music of the pearl disappears too.

Detailed summaries

Chapter 1

Kino the fisherman lives in a little brush house by the sea, with his wife Juana and their firstborn son Coyotito. One perfect morning, Kino wakes up in the dark just before dawn, and listens to the music of the waves beating rhythmically against the beach. In the motion of the sea he hears the Song of the Family. Juana, who has already opened her eyes, looks at Coyotito and then she rekindles the fire for the day's cooking. Kino goes outside to watch the dawn break upon a peaceful morning. The sunlight streams through the cracks in the walls of the brush house. It is a morning like any other morning: the ants are scurrying around, the chickens are having a sham fight, and the pigs are rooting for food. Signs of life from the neighbouring brush houses indicate that others are preparing to start a new day. Kino squats on the ground to eat his usual breakfast of corncake and pulque, which Juana serves him. Juana braids her hair and takes her turn to eat after Kino. They do not speak, as there is no need, and they are content in their silence. One golden sunbeam falls on the box where Coyotito sleeps. Suddenly, Kino and Juana freeze in their positions. A scorpion is moving delicately down the rope which holds up Coyotito's box. Juana mutters an ancient Indian prayer and a Hail Mary, hoping to guard her child against harm. Kino moves stealthily, arms outstretched, ready to sweep the deadly scorpion away. In his mind, he hears the music of the Song of the Enemy. The laughing Coyotito shakes the rope, and the scorpion falls and swiftly stings his shoulder. Coyotito screams. Kino crushes the scorpion to a pulp with his bare hands. Juana lifts the screaming child and tries to suck out the poison from the puncture on his swollen shoulder.

The commotion brings the neighbours crowding to the door of their brush house. They know that a scorpion sting can be fatal to a small baby.

Then Juana, who is normally so patient and obedient, does a surprising thing. She asks for the doctor. This is an amazing thing, for everyone knows that the town doctor will not come to the brush houses, where people cannot afford to pay for his services. Juana is determined that Coyotito will be examined by the doctor. She holds him in a sling made from her tear-stained blue shawl, and leads the way into town for the doctor. Kino follows, and so do all the neighbours. The small procession of people, now joined by others along the way, goes to the edge of the town, where the brush houses give way to stone and plaster houses, with their cool inner gardens. They pass the church, where they are joined by the beggars, who are shrewd observers of men and know that the doctor would never see such poor people as Kino and Juana. They reach the doctor's house at last, where they can hear the singing of caged birds and the smell of bacon frying.

The doctor is having breakfast in bed: hot chocolate in a silver pot, an egg in a delicate cup, and sweet biscuits. He is fat and wealthy, and very discontented with life, as he still longs for Paris, where he once briefly lived. He is not of Kino's race, and Kino feels a smothered rage against this man. For four centuries, Kino's people have been oppressed and despised by the people of the doctor's race. At the doctor's gate, Kino again hears the music of the enemy. Kino knocks on the doctor's gate with his right hand, and with his left removes his hat from his head. The doctor's servant, who is of Kino's race, comes to the gate, but he will not speak to Kino in their old language. He asks Kino to wait while he goes to inform the doctor of Kino's request. As the group of people wait outside the closed gate, the glaring sun throws the shadows of the people on the white walls.

On his master's instructions, the doctor's servant returns to find out if Kino has any money. This time he uses the old language. Kino carefully shows him some ugly, misshapen, and worthless pearls. After reporting to his master again, the servant sends Kino away, but he feels ashamed and quickly shuts the gate. The watching crowd, too, feel the shame spread over them and they melt away quickly. Only Kino and Juana are left at the impressive gates. They stand silently there for a long time. Kino puts his hat back on his head, and then he suddenly strikes the gate fiercely with his bare fist. He stares in amazement at his split knuckles and the blood flowing between his fingers.

NOTES AND GLOSSARY:

the Gulf:	the Gulf of California. La Paz is on the east coast of the Baja California peninsula, facing the mainland
the 'Whole':	the family's whole world; the unity and security of the family's world; also, a reminder of Steinbeck's vision of the wholeness of life
pulque:	a fermented drink made from the sap of an agave plant
Hail Mary:	a Roman Catholic prayer. Juana believes in both the old religion ('ancient magic') of her people, and the Christianity of the Spaniards
lymphatic:	inflamed
Mass:	a religious service of the Roman Catholic church
This doctor was of a race . . .:	this doctor was descended from the Spanish conquerors of Mexico
the old language:	the old Indian language

Chapter 2

The town of old yellow plastered buildings is on an estuary, and the brush houses of the fishing people are clustered near the town. An early morning haze hangs over the whole Gulf, giving the scene a dreamlike quality. Through the haze some things stand out more clearly than others, so that people of the Gulf find difficulty in distinguishing between real images and optical illusions. Thus the Gulf people do not trust what their eyes see and believe more in things of the imagination.

On the beach, dogs and pigs search for food. In the yellow sand of the beach and in the shallow puddles, crabs and small lobsters are scuttling about. Shell and algae border the water's edge. The sea bottom is alive with crawling and swimming and growing things.

In front of the brush huts on the beach, the canoes of the fishermen are drawn up. The canoes are high and graceful, in their blue and white colours. They have been preserved for generations by a hard shell-like plaster. The making of this plaster is the ancient secret of the fishermen.

Kino and his wife walk down the beach to their own canoe, which Kino's grandfather had brought from Nayarit. The canoe has come down to Kino from his father, and it represents both property and a source of food. Kino touches the canoe tenderly, as is his custom. Juana places Coyotito gently in a blanket in the bow of the canoe, and shields him from the sun with her shawl. She makes a poultice of brown seaweed for his swollen shoulder. Then Kino and Juana paddle the canoe rhythmically out into the open waters of the Gulf. The other pearlers have already gathered in their canoes over the oyster beds.

Pearl oysters lie fastened to the bottom of the sea, which is strewn with rubble and the shells of opened oysters. Light filters through the water to reveal grey oysters with encrusted shells. A pearl forms when a grain of sand accidentally falls into an oyster and causes the living oyster to secrete a layer of smooth cement over the irritating sand grain. This process continues until a pearl is formed. Thus some oysters do not hold any pearls, and finding a pearl depends on luck.

Kino dives into the sea. He uses a heavy stone to help him to reach the oyster bed. He has a basket for his collection. He moves carefully in the water so as not to disturb the sand. He is young and strong and can stay below for over two minutes, so he works with deliberate care. In his mind, he hears the Song of the Undersea. Kino's people have made songs of everything that ever existed, and these songs were in the people, even the songs that have been forgotten. Within the Song of the Undersea, Kino faintly hears the secret music of another song; it is the music of the Song of the Pearl That Might Be. In the canoe, Juana prays for the luck to find the oyster; she needs the luck for Coyotito's shoulder.

Kino searches among the closed oysters. Then he sees a partly open shell, very large, and lying by itself under an overhanging rock. He is filled with hope, for he detects a gleam of light in the oyster. Slowly he forces the oyster loose, and swims to the surface with it. He places it in the canoe. He conceals his excitement, but Juana senses it and looks away from him, for wanting a thing too much may drive away the luck.

Kino climbs into the boat, pulls up the stone and the basket, and opens a small oyster first. It is empty and he throws it away. Only then does he look at the large oyster. He knows he may have seen an illusion. Juana softly asks him to open the oyster. Kino skilfully prises open the oyster. In the folds of flesh of the dying oyster lies the great pearl, perfect as the moon, as large as a seagull's egg, and glowing with pure silver light. It is the greatest pearl in the world.

The secret music of the pearl sounds triumphantly in Kino's mind. In the surface of the pearl he can see dream forms. Juana stares at the pearl, which lies in Kino's hand: in the hand that he had smashed against the doctor's closed gate. Instinctively she looks at Coyotito and lifts the seaweed from his shoulder. Coyotito is almost recovered. Seeing this, Kino is so moved that his hand closes over the pearl and he gives a howl to release his pent-up emotions. The men in the other canoes hear Kino, and they race towards his canoe.

NOTES AND GLOSSARY:

mangroves: tropical trees which grow in muddy coastal regions
canoes: light boats
Nayarit: one of the west coast states on the mainland of Mexico, across the Gulf
bulwark: strong defence
mirage: optical illusion
pearlers: pearl divers
a little pat on the back: a reward or encouragement
incandescence: luminous glowing

Chapter 3

The news of Kino's pearl spreads rapidly through the town, and all kinds of people become involved in Kino and his Pearl of the World. The priest wonders if he has baptised Kino's baby. The shopkeepers hope to sell their wares to him. The beggars are thrilled, for they know a poor man who suddenly becomes rich is the best of alms-givers.

When the doctor hears the news, he claims that he is treating Kino's child for a scorpion sting. In his imagination, the doctor is back in Paris, sitting in a restaurant with a bottle of wine.

The pearl buyers hear about Kino's pearl. They are really all agents for only one man, and each person imagines how he can start afresh with new capital; and this capital is somehow linked to Kino's pearl. In fact Kino's pearl plays a new and curious part in the dreams and aspirations of all the people in the town, so that the only obstacle between them and their dreams seems to be Kino. Thus Kino somehow has become every man's enemy. The news of Kino's find stirs up something really evil in the town, and, like venom filling a poison sac, this evil fills and swells the town. But Kino and Juana do not know this.

Kino and Juana think that everyone shares their joy and they plan happily for the future. As the evening sun sinks below the sea, Kino and Juana sit in their brush house and gaze into the pearl, which Kino holds in his hand. The music of the pearl merges with the music of the family, and the two songs beautify each other.

Kino and Juana are surrounded by neighbours, who wonder how any man can have such luck. Juan Tomás, Kino's brother, asks him what he will do now he is a rich man.

Kino and Juana hide their excitement. Kino sees images in the pearl, and he speaks softly about his dreams. Kino and Juana can now be married in church, and Kino sees the stiff new clothes they will wear for the wedding. Then he sees a new harpoon and a rifle.

A rifle is an unbelievable dream. Having said it, all seems possible, for man unlike other creatures has a continual craving for something better. The music of the pearl rises in triumph. Kino has never spoken so many words before, and Juana looks at him in amazement at his courage and imagination.

Kino now utters the impossible dream: his son Coyotito will go to school, and learn all those things which are closed to Kino's people. Through Coyotito, Kino's people too will know and be free. The listening people are hushed. Suddenly, Kino is afraid of all his talking. He closes his hand over the pearl and cuts off its light: his hand is scarred where he had struck the gate with it.

The people know that for them time will now date from Kino's pearl. And whether the pearl brings good or evil to Kino, they will attribute it to that moment when Kino was transformed by his dreams before their very eyes.

It is getting late. Juana begins to make a fire. The people in Kino's hut are reluctant to go home and start their own dinner preparations. Then the priest comes; and Kino again hears the music of the enemy. When Kino shows him the pearl the priest reminds him to give thanks to God who has given him the treasure. Kino is dumbfounded. He is hardly able to make out the invocations of the priest and it is left to Juana to tell the Father of their intention to get married in the church. The priest leaves and the neighbours go home. Kino holds the great pearl in his hand and he is filled with an inexplicable suspicion. Juana boils the beans and makes corn cakes for their dinner. Kino hears the soothing Song of the Family and the familiar domestic sounds give him a sense of security. But looking out into the dark from his door he feels afraid. He has created a future by voicing his plans to the world, and now he has to protect these plans from forces that might destroy them. Deep inside, Kino knows that the gods are angry at men's plans.

As Kino stands thinking, the doctor and his servant come to the door. Kino's cut right hand burns when he sees them, and he is filled with hatred and fear. The doctor moves his black doctor's bag so that Kino will notice it, for he knows that Kino's race trusts the tools of any craft. He pretends that he has come at the first opportunity to examine Kino's baby. He insinuates that a scorpion sting is tricky and causes death unexpectedly. Kino is trapped by ignorance and fear for his son's life, so he allows the doctor and the servant to enter his house.

Juana too is reluctant to allow the doctor access to her child, and relents only when Kino indicates his approval. The doctor examines Coyotito in the light of the lantern held by his servant. Holding the baby's eyelid down he insists that it is blue and that the poison is in the child, ready to strike. He feeds the child some white powder, and goes, promising to be back within an hour. After the doctor has gone, Kino notices the pearl in his hand. He wraps it in a rag and buries it in the dirt floor of his hut.

At home, the doctor has a meal of chocolate, sweet cakes, and fruit. In the estuary outside Kino's house, a school of small fishes tries frantically to escape the great fishes that are pursuing them. In their brush houses, the people can hear the slaughter in the river.

Kino squats by the fire to a dinner of boiled beans and corn cake. He has just finished and is rolling himself a cigarette when Coyotito becomes very sick. The baby has stomach spasms and vomits, writhing in his mother's arms. Kino is alarmed, but cannot help being suspicious of the powder that was fed to his baby by the doctor. The neighbours come around offering aid and comfort in their own way. Juana moans out the Song of the Family as though it could save Coyotito.

Then the doctor arrives. He gives the baby some drops of ammonia in a glass of water. He waits till the spasms subside and the baby falls asleep. He claims to have cured the child and asks when Kino will pay.

Kino replies that he will pay after he has sold the pearl. At this juncture the doctor looks surprised. He says that he has not heard about the pearl and offers to keep it in his safe for Kino. He adds that it would be a shame to have the pearl stolen before it could be sold. All this time his eyes never leave Kino's face and he sees Kino look involuntarily to the spot where the pearl is buried. The doctor leaves and the neighbours return to their huts. Kino stands uneasily at the door of his house. The music of evil sounds in his head and he is afraid. He reburies the pearl in a new place. Juana watches him and finally asks him whom he fears. Kino replies, 'Everyone.' He feels a hardness growing over him.

The whole family sleeps on a mat on the floor that night. Kino has a troubled sleep with the music of evil playing in his dream. He awakens and hears soft sounds in the darkness of the hut. Juana lays a warning hand on him, but Kino leaps at the intruder. He strikes the intruder with his knife, and is himself hit on the head. Juana calls to him in terror and Kino tells her that 'the thing' has gone. Juana lights a candle and tends to the cut on Kino's head. Hate is growing in Kino. In great fear, Juana tells Kino that the pearl is like a sin, which will destroy them. She wants Kino to get rid of it. Kino is determined that they will have their one chance for a better life; Coyotito will go to school. Then he notices the bloody knife in his hands, and he plunges it into the earth to clean it.

Dawn is almost breaking. Kino digs up the pearl and gazes at it. Its loveliness comforts him and he relaxes and smiles. Juana, seeing him smile, is gladdened; and so they begin the second day with hope.

NOTES AND GLOSSARY:

colonial animal: either an animal (like coral or sponge) which, while resembling one organism, is actually made up of many independent individual animals; or animals that live in organised groups (like ants and termites)

a curious dark residue was precipitated: a strange and evil result was produced

the Peninsula: Lower California, which is divided into two parts. The northern half belongs to the United States and the southern half to Mexico ('Territorio de Baja California')

the outward sea: Pacific Ocean

a man transfigured: a man amazingly changed

a great Father of the Church: Eusebio Francisco Kino (1645–1711), a Jesuit missionary in Lower California, who worked among the Indians

consecrated candle: a candle blessed by the Church, to be used for religious purposes

cleansed: cleaned; also has the suggestion of purification

cozened: deceived

Chapter 4

A little town has its own way of keeping track of itself and all its units, especially where one of these units steps out of its regular and well-known pattern. Then the town people get nervous and this nervousness is communicated to the whole town.

Thus on the day that Kino intends to sell his pearl, the whole town wakes early in anticipation. Word of the occasion spreads to the pearl fishermen and Chinese grocers, to nuns and beggars, and most of all to the pearl buyers.

Each pearl buyer sits alone in his office, to give the impression that there are many separate traders. In reality, all the pearl buyers represent just one man, and they already know how the other buyers will bid.

On this special day, the sun is hot yellow in the uncertain light of the Gulf, and a vision of a distant mountain hangs in the air. The fishermen have not gone out in their canoes, for they do not want to miss the excitement. Lingering over their breakfasts, they discuss what they would each do if the pearl was theirs: give it as a present to the Pope; buy Masses for a thousand years; give the money to the poor of La Paz; perform all the good deeds possible. All the neighbours hope that the pearl will not destroy Kino, for he and his family are well-liked.

For Kino and Juana this is the turning-point of their lives. Coyotito is dressed in his baptismal clothes by his mother. Juana braids her hair and Kino wears his clean though ragged clothes. He imagines that this is the last time that he will be wearing his rags.

The neighbours are dressed and ready also. They will accompany Kino on this historic occasion. Not going would be a sign of 'unfriendship'.

Juana puts on her head shawl and carries Coyotito in a hammock made from the long end of it. She carries him thus so he can see the proceedings and perhaps remember them. Kino's hat sits on his head, slightly tilted forward to indicate aggressiveness and seriousness and vigour. The great pearl is wrapped in a piece of deerskin and placed in a leather bag carried in Kino's shirt pocket. Kino steps out of the house with dignity. Juana follows, carrying Coyotito. As they march towards town, a huge crowd of people follow. But because this is a serious occasion, only Kino's older brother, Juan Tomás, walks with him.

Juan Tomás warns Kino nervously against being cheated. He tells Kino that, before Kino was born, the villagers once made a plan to entrust their pearls to an agent who would sell them in the capital and retain only his share of the profits. Twice they appointed an agent, and both times the agent disappeared with the pearls. So they have given up and gone back to the old way. Kino has heard the story from his father. The priest has preached on it many times too and has made it clear that the loss of the pearls was punishment meted out to the people for trying to leave their station in life, and move away from the slot in which God had placed them. As the brothers walk along they squint their eyes in the custom of their people. The squint and a slight tightening of their lips are their only defence against their powerful oppressors, for they can withdraw completely behind this wall of reticence.

The solemn procession of people goes past the brush houses and enters the city. More people join it: beggars, grocers, drinkers from the saloons. The sun shines hotly down, so that even the tiny stones throw dark shadows on the ground. The pearl buyers get ready in their gloomy offices with barred windows.

The first pearl buyer whom Kino sees looks like a fatherly, kind, and friendly man. Close-shaven and clean, he sits behind his desk. He secretly practises a skilful little coin trick with his right hand behind his desk. As he hears the crowd approaching, his hand moves faster and faster.

Kino enters the dim little office and the pearl buyer looks at him with steady, cruel, and unwinking eyes, while his right hand continues with its secret little trick. The crowd looks through the doorway. Kino quietly tells the buyer that he has a pearl, and the buyer pretends to be uninterested. Then Kino dramatically produces his pearl and looks at the buyer's face. The buyer's face does not change, but his right hand falters in its coin trick. The buyer takes out his right hand and handles the pearl. Kino waits tensely, while the crowd whispers excitedly behind him.

The pearl buyer tosses the pearl into the tray on his desk, and contemptuously dismisses it as fool's gold: of no value because its large size makes it a freak, a thing of curiosity only. He offers one thousand pesos for it. Kino is puzzled at first and then filled with anger. He knows he is being cheated, for the great pearl is worth at least fifty thousand pesos. The crowd becomes discontented. Sensing this, the buyer is frightened and offers to let other pearl buyers evaluate the pearl. To prove his honesty, he elaborately sends for three other pearl buyers. Then he pulls out another coin and continues his mechanical coin trick, but he cannot take his eyes off the pearl in front of him. The crowd begins to feel that the pearl buyer is honest and that Kino should accept his offer. But Kino helplessly feels the evil growing upon him, and hears the music of evil. Only the presence of Juana strengthens him.

Three more pearl dealers come through the silent, watching crowd into the first dealer's office. All of them pretend that they are not accomplices in the plot to cheat Kino. The first of the new buyers dismisses the pearl with contempt. The second one examines the pearl more carefully and says that its quality is poor. The third man offers five hundred pesos. Kino snatches up his pearl and tells the pearl buyers he will sell his pearl elsewhere, perhaps in the capital. The dealers are dismayed and afraid. The man behind the desk quickly raises his offer to fifteen hundred pesos. But the angry Kino is leaving already, with Juana behind him.

That evening, the people of the brush houses discuss the great event of the morning. They are unwilling to admit that the dealers could have arranged the whole thing secretly, for admitting it would mean that all of them have been cheated all their lives.

While they discuss Kino's actions, Kino himself broods in his own house. He has lost one world and has not gained another. He has buried the pearl under a stone in the fire hole of his house. Visions of the faraway capital terrify him. The thought of leaving the familiarity of his world for the unknown capital is frightening. He has never been far from home before. If he decides not to go, he will be destroying the future he has promised himself. He has said he will go, and saying it is to be halfway there. Juana watches him silently while she attends to her household duties.

Juan Tomás comes to sympathise with Kino. As Juan Tomás is older, Kino seeks his advice. He tells Kino that although they are cheated all their lives, they still survive. Kino's defiance in the morning is not just against the pearl dealers. It is against the whole structure of their world. Juan Tomás warns Kino that he is going towards greater danger, and he will be going without friends. But the great sense of outrage in Kino will not allow him to turn back now. They part with a sense of fear between them.

Kino continues his brooding. He feels hopelessness settling upon him. The dark music of the enemy resounds in his head. He hears in his despair the movements of animals, the little waves on the beach and other night sounds. Juana watches him and knows she can help him best by being silent and by being near. She sings softly the Song of the Family as if to fight the other song, the Song of Evil. She sings the song to Coyotito to keep the evil out. Kino does not ask for his supper. He sits entranced by the little fire in their home. He senses the evil outside the brush house and feels that dark creeping things are waiting for him to go out into the night. Feeling threatened and challenged, he touches the knife in his shirt. Juana raises her hand to stop him, but he has gone into the darkness. She picks up a stone and follows him, but the night attackers have already left and Kino is alone, bleeding and barely conscious. She helps him into the house.

Juana begs Kino to destroy the pearl quickly before it destroys them. Kino refuses as he is determined to succeed. He tells her that they will leave in their canoe the next morning and sell the pearl in the capital.

NOTES AND GLOSSARY:

La Paz: the biggest town in the southern part of Lower California, situated on La Paz Bay

tithe: religious tax, here meaning charitable offering

many hands: many dealers working for one man

vision of a mountain: the Sierra de la Giganta mountain range, north of La Paz

the Holy Father in Rome: the Pope, the head of the Roman Catholic church

the capital: Mexico City, on the mainland

visited: inflicted

legerdemain: sleight of hand, conjuring trick

understatement: statement which deliberately minimises the importance of something

fool's gold: iron pyrites; something which only appears valuable

collusion: secret cooperation for a dishonest purpose

a glass: magnifying glass

the game: the scheme, the undertaking, followed up like a game

lethargy: weariness, apathy

entranced: enraptured, dazed

Chapter 5

Kino opens his eyes in the darkness. He remains motionless, for he senses movement near him. And in the pale moonlight that filters through the chinks in the brush house he sees Juana move towards the fireplace. Very carefully, she moves the fireplace stone. Then she glides towards the door, only pausing a moment at Coyotito's box, and is gone. In a rage, Kino goes after his wife. She runs towards the sea and raises her arm to throw the pearl back into the water. Kino wrenches the pearl from her. He strikes her in the face and she falls among the rocks. Then he kicks her in the side. He hisses like a snake through his bared teeth, but Juana is unafraid, lying at the water's edge with the little waves breaking over her. Like a sheep before the butcher, she is mute and unprotesting. The rage within Kino gives way to disgust. He turns and walks away.

As he walks up the brush line he is attacked. He plunges his knife into a dark figure. Then he is overpowered. Greedy fingers frantically search through his clothes as he lies helpless on the ground. The pearl, knocked from his hand, lies a little behind the pathway, glinting softly in the moonlight.

Juana drags herself up from the beach. Her senses are dulled with pain, but she feels no anger for Kino. He has said, 'I am a man.' For her, the words mean that he is half insane and half god. He would pit his strength against overwhelming odds even if the attempt killed him. She cannot understand these things, but she can accept them, and she needs them. She knows, too, that sometimes the qualities of a woman, reason and caution and the sense of preservation, can cut through a man's madness and save them all.

She walks slowly up the path towards her house. The fitful light of the moon reveals the glimmer of the pearl lying on the path and for a moment Juana thinks of throwing it into the sea. Then she sees two dark figures: Kino, and a man with blood flowing from his throat and Kino's knife next to him. Instantly, Juana knows the old life is gone for ever, and that there is nothing to do but to save themselves. She hides the dead man in the brush and revives Kino. She convinces Kino that they must all flee. He sends her to get Coyotito from the house while he fetches the canoe.

Going back to the beach as dawn rises Kino sees that his ancient canoe has been smashed. This is an evil act. Kino must flee like an animal, but he never thinks of stealing one of his neighbours' canoes. Hurrying back to his house, he sees flames in the sky: his house is on fire. Juana comes with the terrified baby in her arms, and tells him that 'the dark ones' have started the fire.

The neighbours hurry out to watch, and to stamp out the sparks that threaten to set their own houses alight. Kino is suddenly afraid. The light makes him afraid. Light is dangerous to him as he remembers the man he has slain. He quickly draws Juana to the shadows and makes his way in the dark to Juan Tomás's house. From there they watch their house burn to ashes. They see, through the spaces in the brush wall, the commotion around the burnt-out house. The neighbours think Kino's family is dead. Apolonia as chief female relative raises a formal lament for the dead. But Apolonia has only her second-best head shawl so she rushes into her house to get her fine new one. Kino confronts her as she looks for her shawl. He tells her not to raise the alarm and to get Juan Tomás but no one else. Juan Tomás comes and Kino tells him how he has killed a man. Juan Tomás immediately traces the cause of their plight to the evil pearl. He agrees worriedly to hide the desperate Kino and his family for a day.

They sit silently in the house all day. They can see the neighbours rummaging in the ashes looking for their bones. They sense the shock when the neighbours discover Kino's canoe smashed. Juan Tomás diverts attention from his own house and is among the neighbours, suggesting that Kino might have found another boat, or gone south to escape the evil.

The Gulf wind rises and screams through La Paz, so that Juan Tomás can say to the neighbours that Kino must be drowned in the bay. He brings food, water, and a heavy knife to Kino, who plans to go north where there are cities. Kino tells his brother bitterly that he will keep the pearl because it has become his misfortune and his life. As Kino says this, Coyotito whimpers and Juana comforts him with her ancient prayers.

They leave in the dark that night before moonrise. Kino and his brother embrace each other and Kino says again that the pearl has become his soul.

NOTES AND GLOSSARY:

leprosy: a loathsome wasting disease: Kino has become something to be shunned

little magics: prayers from the old Indian religion (like the 'ancient magic' of Chapter 1)

Chapter 6

Kino and Juana gather their clothes tightly about them as they walk out into the world. The fierce wind pelts them with bits of twigs and stones. They tread their way around the town, avoiding the centre where they might be seen, and start along the sandy road leading to Loreto.

The wind is strong and Kino knows that it will wipe out his tracks. But he is fearful of the dark and the devils that haunt the night. Yet through this fear he feels a rush of exhilaration that makes him cautious and wary and dangerous. Some ancient animal thing out of the past of his people is alive in him as he walks carefully, with Juana behind him.

The moon rises when they are a good distance away from the town. The wind subsides, but Kino keeps to the track, knowing that their footprints will be wiped out by the carts going to the town in the morning. They walk all through the night. Kino walks carefully in a wheel rut and Juana follows in his path. He grips the handle of his big knife and tries to draw some protection from it.

The night owl screeches and hisses over their heads and a coyote laughs in the brush. The music of the pearl is triumphant in Kino's ears. Underlying it is the music of the family. Kino and Juana walk till early dawn. Then Kino finds a covert hidden from the road and settles Juana in the hidden clearing. He himself goes back to sweep the place where their footprints lead away from the sandy road. Having done that he returns to the covert and waits. Juana feeds Coyotito. Then as dawn begins to break, a cart goes by, wiping out their footprints.

Juana gives Kino the corn cakes that Apolonia has packed. Then she sleeps. Kino does not sleep. He sits staring at the ground, and watches as a column of ants climbs over his foot, which he had put in their path, and continues on its way.

The sun is high and hot when Juana wakes. Kino warns her about things she already knows: the tree that can blind a person who touches it, and the tree that bleeds and brings bad luck. They talk about the pearl.

Kino takes the pearl out and looks into it to find his vision. He looks into the pearl to see his rifle and sees instead a dark body lying dead on the road. Taken aback, Kino quickly tells Juana that they will be married in a great church, and in the pearl he sees Juana, her face swollen from his blows, crawling home in the night. Frantically he looks into the pearl for a vision of Coyotito learning to read. Instead, he sees his baby's face, thick and feverish from the white powder the doctor has given him. Kino shoves the pearl back into his shirt and the music of the pearl sounds sinister in his ears. The music of the pearl is interwoven with the music of evil.

The sun beats down and it is very hot. Kino relaxes and sleeps with his hat over his eyes. Juana sits, quiet as a stone, and keeps watch. Coyotito wakes and Juana plays happily with him. She gives him a little water, and as she does so, Kino stirs in a dream. He moans and sits up suddenly, eyes bright and nostrils flared like a nervous animal. He tests the edge of his knife and tells Juana to keep Coyotito quiet. Then he makes his way to the edge of the road. He hides behind a thorny tree and scrutinises the way by which they have come.

In the distance he sees three figures, two on foot and one on horseback. He knows they are trackers. These inland hunters who survive because of their tremendous skill at tracking are hunting him now. Kino watches, his body stiff with caution and fear as the trackers bend low to the ground, whining like excited dogs warming to the trail.

Kino draws his big knife in readiness. He knows that if the trackers find him now his only chance will be to kill the horseman and grab his rifle.

Coyotito gurgles and Juana quickly feeds him to keep him quiet. The trackers come near. The horse flings up its head and snorts. The trackers try to interpret the horse's ears, and then they move away, slowly.

Kino dashes back to where Juana is hiding. He does not attempt to cover his tracks as there are too many signs to hide. He is in panic flight. For a moment, he hesitates, uncertain whether he should give himself up. His hand touches the pearl hidden under his shirt.

Juana watches Kino and reminds him that the trackers will not let any of them live after they take the pearl. Kino is overpowered by helplessness, but Juana's goading rouses him.

The couple are frantic as they gather the little bundles of food and water. They make their way to the high stone mountain. In the panic, there is no time to cover tracks nor to conceal their passage. The sun streams down as they flee to the great mountain which stands like a refuge for pursued animals.

The countryside leading to the mountain is waterless and rocky. The family moves through this barren terrain of dry grass and cacti. In his mind Kino knows that the trackers will find them sooner or later. The music of evil sings loudly in Kino's head with the whine of the heat and the sound of snakes rattling. The song is not overwhelming, but secret and poisonous.

The terrain of broken rock gives way to greater slabs of rock rising towards the mountain. Here they rest for a while behind a large boulder on a slope. Juana gives Coyotito some water and the parched baby drinks greedily. Kino meanwhile climbs to the top of the rock. He sees that his enemies are not yet in sight, and he climbs down to join Juana.

He suggests to Juana that he should lead the trackers into the mountain while she hides. When the trackers eventually leave, she could go on to Loreto where he would join her later. But Juana shows no sign of weakness or irresolution and refuses to leave Kino. Kino takes strength from her steadfastness and when they move on again there is no panic.

The country rising towards the mountain consists of long granite outcrops with deep crevices between them. Kino leaps from ledge to ledge on the unmarkable stone. He does not take a straight path but zigzags and circles and double-tracks in his attempt to leave the trackers a difficult trail.

They make their way towards a dark cleft in the mountain, hoping to find much-needed water. The stream in the cleft starts high in the range and flows in a trickle down the smooth rock. Here and there the water collects in shallow pools. The stream continues down the mountainside forming a series of pools, until it disappears into the dry rubble at the foot of the mountain.

Wild animals come to these little pools to drink: wild sheep and deer and puma and birds. At the sides of the pools colonies of plants grow, wherever there is enough soil. Insects and frogs live in the water. The pools support life because of the water. But they are places of death too. Cats sometimes prey on the animals that come to drink.

Kino and Juana are exhausted when they arrive at the last pool. Juana, although weary herself, washes Coyotito's face first and gives him a drink from her freshly filled bottle. The weary baby cries softly till Juana feeds him. Kino takes a long drink, then stretches out to relax, but only for a little while. He is up again scanning the horizon. And far down the slope he sees the trackers. The distance makes them small and they appear like two scurrying ants followed by a larger ant, the horseman.

Kino stiffens and Juana notices it. He looks up and quickly makes his way to some small caves about thirty feet above the pool. Each cave is only a few feet deep and slopes down towards the back. Kino tells Juana she must hide in the cave. Juana obeys. He helps her up and passes their provisions up to her.

While Juana watches, Kino climbs up another hundred feet to the next step in the mountain. He claws at the plants and deliberately makes his passage clear. He hopes that the trackers will follow this false trail and miss their cave. Then he climbs down and tells Juana his plan for them to slip away when the trackers take the trail up the mountain. He cautions her to keep Coyotito quiet and Juana replies, as she looks into the baby's solemn eyes, that Coyotito knows.

It is twilight when the trackers finally arrive at the pool which Kino and Juana have left. They look up and see the tracks going up the cliff. But they do not follow. They light their cigarettes and sit down to eat. Darkness falls, and the animals that come to the pool move away when they smell man. Coyotito whimpers and Juana covers his head with her shawl to muffle him. One of the pursuers lights a match and Kino sees, in the flare, that two of the men are sleeping. Only the man holding the rifle keeps watch. A plan forms in his mind and he whispers quietly to Juana that he will kill the man with the rifle first. The sleeping ones can be dealt with later. Juana is afraid that they will see his white clothes in the starlight. Kino then explains that he has to do it before the moon rises. He cannot find a softer word to say to Juana so he says that if he is killed, she should lie quietly and make for Loreto when the men leave. Her voice trembles when she bids him, 'Go with God.'

Kino looks tenderly at his wife. He places his hand on Coyotito's head. Then he touches Juana's cheek and prepares to go. Juana sees Kino take off his white clothes and hang the long knife on his amulet string. She peers out from the cave entrance. She carries the sleeping Coyotito and whispers a combination of native magic and Hail Marys to ward off the evil. The night seems less dark as she looks at it. The moon has not yet risen but already begins to light up a small patch of sky. She sees also the light from the cigarette of the waiting man below.

Kino spreads his whole body against the face of the mountain and moves down with extreme care, limb by limb like a lizard. He cannot afford to make a single sound or dislodge the smallest pebble, as that would alert the enemy. The night, however, is not silent. The tree frogs and cicadas are singing their own songs. These sounds mingle with the Song of the Family which is alive in Kino. The family song is fierce and strong and suppresses the music of the enemy which is also in him. As Kino moves down he breathes with his mouth open so that even his breath has no sound. Kino takes a long time to reach the bottom, and when he does, he crouches behind a dwarf palm to catch his breath.

He is only twenty feet from the enemy now. He looks warily at the place where the moon will rise. Then he looks for the man who is keeping watch. But as he takes the great knife from his neck, the moon rises and Kino has to hide behind the bush again.

He is too late. He sees the enemy light a cigarette and waits for him to turn his face. He must strike without hesitation when the man turns. And Kino waits, his body coiled and ready to strike. Just then, the sound of a murmuring cry reaches the men. One of the sleepers awakes and sits up. He and the watcher try to decide whether a coyote or a human baby is responsible for the noise. The sound comes again and this time the watcher takes his gun and shoots in the direction of the cave above the hills. Kino leaps as the gun goes off. He is like a terrible machine. He kills the man with the gun and wrenches the gun from him. Then he turns and kills the other two men deliberately.

Kino is as cold and deadly as steel. But something bothers him. He is uncertain what to do. The tree frogs are silent and the cicadas are still. Something is trying to reach him. His tension begins to fade and then he hears, coming from the cave above, the cry of death.

Everyone in La Paz remembers the return of Kino's family. The older people had seen it with their own eyes, and others not so old were told the story by their fathers and grandfathers. It was late one beautiful afternoon at sunset, and the shadows were long. Perhaps the shadows made people remember.

Kino and Juana walk into the city from the country road. They walk side by side, and not, as usual, with Kino in front and Juana behind. Kino has a rifle across his arm. Juana carries a small limp bundle in her shawl, slung across her shoulder. The shawl is crusted with dried blood and the bundle sways a little as she walks. Juana's face is hard and tight with fatigue. She is withdrawn and remote and her eyes stare inward into herself. Kino seems to be in a dangerous mood, with his jaw set and his lips thin and hard.

Juana and her husband walk with the sun behind them and their shadows, like two towers of darkness, stride before them. They seem to be protected by some magic, for people let them pass, and make way for them. The pearl dealers in the city peer at them behind barred windows. Mothers hide their children's faces. People who have rushed to meet them stand back to let them pass, and even Juan Tomás withholds his greetings.

Kino and Juana walk through the town, seeing nothing, staring straight ahead. The Song of the Family burns fiercely in Kino's ear like a battle cry. They walk unseeingly past their burnt-out house and at the beach, they ignore the broken canoe. At the water's edge, Kino puts his rifle down. From his clothes, he takes out the pearl. He looks at it and it is grey and ulcerous. In the dark glimmer of the pearl he sees the eyes of the man at the pool. And he sees little Coyotito, with the top of his head blown off, lying in the mountain cave. He hears the music of the pearl, and it is distorted and insane. Trembling a little, Kino holds the pearl out to Juana. She looks at it for a moment, and says softly, 'No, you'.

With all his strength, Kino flings the pearl far out into the sea. As it falls, the pearl glimmers in the sun and Kino and Juana, standing side by side, watch for a long time the spot where it made a splash in the water.

The pearl settles into the water. The greenish sheen on its surface is very beautiful. It rests among the fern-like plants at the bottom of the sea, and is covered with sand by a little scuttling crab, and then it is gone. The music of the pearl, soft as a whisper, disappears.

NOTES AND GLOSSARY:

Loreto:	a town about 150 miles north of La Paz
trackers:	hunters who are expert in following animal trails
goading:	urging a person on
monolithic:	formed of a single block of stone
Santa Rosalia:	a town about 250 miles north of La Paz
ancient intercession:	prayers in Juana's old Indian religion (like her 'ancient magic' in Chapter 1)
germane:	appropriate
cicadas:	winged insects
coyote:	North American prairie wolf. The word ironically suggests Coyotito, which means 'little coyote'
immune:	protected; exempt or free from danger

Part 3

Commentary

THE STYLE AND MEANING OF *The Pearl* cannot easily be separated from each other, for in any novel, style and content are inextricably bound and reinforce each other. The meaning of *The Pearl* can be seen in the pattern or structure of the book, for this ordering of materials has been determined by the author's vision of life. Bearing this qualification in mind, though, it is convenient to isolate certain features of the book for the purposes of detailed study.

The nature of *The Pearl*

Steinbeck's story of the pearl is a greatly expanded version of the original folk-tale which he heard in La Paz, Mexico, in 1940. In his introduction to *The Pearl*, Steinbeck calls his story a parable, implying that it is a rather simple narrative with a moral meaning to be derived from it. Such a view is undoubtedly true, but it grossly simplifies the scope of Steinbeck's changes to the Indian folk-story. These changes lengthen the original 350-word story to one of about 30,000 words. Steinbeck's version contains more complex characters, a vivid sense of locality, and various stylistic devices that complicate the meaning of the story. In this way, he has transformed *The Pearl* into a realistic narrative with sharp sociological analysis, as well as made it into a timeless and universal story about the human condition. Stylistically too, *The Pearl* combines realism with lyricism, while its essential simplicity makes it a haunting story of Everyman,* of mankind in general.

The subtly fused realistic and lyrical nature of *The Pearl* permeates the very quality of life in La Paz, so that the ordinary things of life lose their distinct shapes and become insubstantial. In such a dreamlike atmosphere, the people of the Gulf can easily believe that their world mingles with the world of the spirit.

> The uncertain air that magnified some things and blotted out others hung over the whole Gulf so that all sights were unreal and vision could not be trusted . . . Thus it might be that the people of the Gulf trust things of the spirit and things of the imagination (pp.13–14).

The image of the hazy mirage that Steinbeck has created here is also

* *Everyman* was a fifteenth-century play which dealt with the theme of death and the fate of man's soul.

an image of his stylistic technique. Things become unreal to the outward eye, and take on the symbolic meaning of inner vision. Kino is aware, when he sees the pearl, that he might have found a complete illusion, for 'in this Gulf of uncertain light there were more illusions than realities' (p.19).

The appearance of the pearl intensifies the ambiguity of illusion. It is perfect as the moon and its light is a pure silver incandescence. Kino gazes at its perfect beauty in a state of near trance, seeming to see the dream forms of the future on its glowing surface. The pearl is lovely, but what Kino sees is not the objective loveliness of the pearl. He sees his own secret desires mirrored in the perfect illusion of the pearl.

Steinbeck contrasts the illusory promise of the pearl with the reality of life which surrounds it. The immediate reality around the discovery of the pearl has an aura of death. The pearl is plucked from the 'dying flesh' (p.19) of the oyster; the pearl is held by Kino in the hand he has smashed against the doctor's gate, and the torn flesh of the knuckles is grey from the seawater. The torn and dying flesh of reality serves as a reminder of the harsh conditions of Kino's past life, and as a premonition of the suffering and death that will come in the future.

The Pearl as a social document

Two approaches: science and philosophy

Time and place are felt strongly in most of Steinbeck's novels. The early works evoke an intensely vivid picture of California. This element of his style is indispensable in his examination of life, for it gives sharpness of focus to his critique. Time and place are no less precisely recorded in *The Pearl*, making it a valuable sociological study.

Steinbeck has rooted his story firmly in a particularised setting, La Paz on the Gulf of California, with the desert and mountains behind it. It is the story of a community made up of a Spanish-Mexican town, with a small Indian-Mexican fishing village huddled around the outskirts of the town. Steinbeck has also given the story a specific time, unlike the original folk-tale, which takes place over an indeterminate length of time. *The Pearl* covers a period of five days, each one well defined, with the narrative opening at dawn of the first day and closing at dusk on the last.

Most of the sociological data in the realistic background of the novella was collected by Steinbeck from personal visits to Mexico. He had visited that country briefly in 1935 after writing *Tortilla Flat* (which is about Mexicans living in America). In 1940, he chartered a boat, the *Western Flyer*, and made a leisurely trip along the coast of the Gulf of

California. The aim of the trip, which covered six weeks in March and April of 1940, was to collect marine specimens from the Gulf, make observations about the settlements along the coastal regions, gather information about the tides of the Gulf, and hold long conversations with Ed Ricketts about life in general. Steinbeck hoped that the combination of scientific and philosophical enquiries would enable them to study the human race as a species, and to discover traits that were as distinctly patterned as those of any other biological species.

The Pearl reflects the dual concerns, scientific and philosophical, recorded in *The Log from the Sea of Cortez*. With the accuracy of the eye of a camera, Steinbeck records the action; with the central intelligence of the omniscient author, he interprets those actions in accordance with his vision of life. The two approaches are combined in the sociological study of a small community on the Gulf of California.

Social tensions of La Paz

The community of La Paz, as described in *The Pearl*, is a closed, complete, and self-sufficient society. This society has a rigid structure, its social ranks immovably tiered. It has been like this since the time of the Spanish conquest, during the hundreds of years of subjugation which have been sanctified by religion. It is a society based on racial and economic antagonism between wealthy Spaniards and poor Indians. Those Indians who, before Kino was born, tried to change the system failed miserably. Like Kino, they had conceived the idea of selling their pearls in the capital for a better price. The Indians sent their own agents to the capital, but these agents had vanished without a trace. In despair, the Indians gave up and went back to 'the old way' (p.43). The priest drove home the lesson against rebellion by an annual sermon, which stressed the wickedness of leaving one's predetermined place in this world, as 'it was against religion' (p.43).

In this smaller version of the tale of Kino's pearl lies the gist of Steinbeck's critical appraisal of the nature of life in La Paz. Society is built on inequality, an inequality of race, economics, and religion; and the static system is fostered by keeping the Indians subordinate in their fear, ignorance, and superstition. Kino's wish to educate his son shows his courage and his imagination. Education is the magnificent symbol of freedom. As Kino says, 'these things [learning to read and write] will make us free because he [Coyotito] will know—he will know and through him we will know' (p.25). But because they do not 'know' and are afraid, the Indians are unaware that their priest has corrupted his religious teachings in order to safeguard his own social position; and Kino and Juana can be trapped into permitting the greedy and callous doctor to poison their son.

The village

The simple way of life of the Indian fishing village is never idealised. The authenticity of Steinbeck's sociological study is manifested in his keen attention to detail: the ragged, clean clothes, the poor interiors of the brush houses, the monotonous simplicity of the food, the unvarying routine of their days, and even the description of the scratching chickens in the dust outside.

The Indian way of life is a hard one, and yet it is not without beauty and dignity. Kino and Juana, though poor, are very much in love and are obviously happy and thrilled with their first-born child. Their unspoken sense of peace with each other contrasts vividly with the doctor's dissatisfaction with his own life.

There is a fundamental simplicity in this Indian way of life. In all that the Indians do, there is a pervading sense of the immemorial quality of their existence. They are so close to nature that they seem to be a human extension of the ancient land; and their gods are the ancient heathen gods before the time of the Spanish conquerors. Juana's prayers are a blend of ancient rituals and Christian formulas. The rhythm of their lives is the natural rhythm of the cycle of day-and-night. When they go into the desert, they go with a minimum of bare essentials: water and food, and Juana suckles her baby naturally. In the desert, the ancient quality of the Indians comes to the surface. As Kino leads the way into the dark night, 'some ancient thing out of the past of his people' (p.65) is alive in him.

The profoundly ancient quality of life in the Indians has been transmitted through the generations in the symbolic form of the canoe. Kino's canoe came from Nayarit. It was very old and had come down to Kino from his grandfather. It was 'property and source of food' (p.14): symbol of social wealth and still utilitarian. It was yet something more. Every year Kino 'refinished his canoe . . . by the secret method' (p.14) of his family; and Kino's relationship with his canoe was tender, and almost mystical. The canoe represented the richness of the past in Kino's present life.

The Pearl, then, presents not just a realistic picture of social conditions. It has the added depth of an understanding of the anthropological origins of such conditions. In making his sociological observations, Steinbeck is always profoundly aware of the human proportions of life.

Sensitivity for the characters can be seen in the indirect expression of emotion in the tense relationship between the Indian-Mexicans and the Spanish-Mexicans. Kino's people have learned to disguise the antagonism they feel for their oppressors; perhaps, after hundreds of years, they are barely conscious of the tension. Kino's hesitation at the doctor's gate arises from the rage and terror that he feels for people of the doctor's race. Kino does not fully comprehend the nature of his feelings; he only knows that he hears the music of the enemy and that 'he could kill the doctor more easily than he could talk to him' (p.9).

He feels a similar reaction to the priest. However, Kino and his people have learned that their only defence is to withdraw from the aggression of their oppressors, and not to reveal their secret feelings. Their only visible reaction is 'a slight slitting of the eyes and a slight tightening of the lips and a retirement' (p.43–44).

The town

In contrast to the simplicity of the fishing village, the town dwellers lead a relatively sophisticated life. They are represented by the wealthier and more influential sections of the community, such as the doctor and the priest, and to a lesser extent by the pearl buyers. There are also the beggars who laze in the shadow of the church all day, but who, in reality, are shrewd observers of life. La Paz gives the impression of a bustling town, although Steinbeck describes in detail only a few of its more prominent citizens.

The sense of community relationships can be felt not just in the scenes of the busy town, but also in the description of village life. Steinbeck achieves the effect of communality in two ways.

Firstly, he suggests the sense of excitement that can sweep mysteriously through a community. Juana, taking her baby to the doctor, heads a procession of friends and neighbours who have quickly gathered at the first sign of something unusual taking place. The procession, with 'all the neighbours [and] the children trotting on the flanks' (p.8), passes the fringes of the brush houses, the outer city walls, and the cool inner gardens: the image evokes a sense of people, of movement, and of buildings laid out in the characteristic manner of Mexican towns. Steinbeck draws a picture of the group, the community, with a life and impetus of its own, to enlarge our impression of La Paz. Secondly, he analyses the nature of the inner relationships within the community.

A town is a thing like a colonial animal. A town has a nervous system . . . And a town has a whole emotion . . . The nerves of the town were vibrating with the news . . . The news swept on past the brush houses, and it washed in a foaming wave into the town of stone and plaster (p.21).

In this analysis, Steinbeck stresses the analogy between a town and an organic or living thing (in words like 'colonial animal', 'nervous system', 'emotion', and 'foaming wave'). By this method, he suggests an aliveness in the town which contributes to the picture of a stirring, eventful society.

The idea of the town as a living organism is also of thematic significance. The people of La Paz form a society whose parts are affected by
every other part. Part of Steinbeck's criticism is directed towards those
who are blind to the needs of others within their community. La Paz
is a living organism in the sense that a disease in one of its parts will
affect every other part. The image of groups of people forming, and
becoming, a living unit is essential to Steinbeck's concept of the organic
community. The discovery of the pearl, therefore, affects not only
Kino, but the whole population of La Paz; the priest, the doctor, the
neighbours, the shopkeepers, the beggars, 'every man suddenly became
related to Kino's pearl' (p.22).

La Paz is an old city (as Steinbeck informs us in *The Log from the Sea
of Cortez**), whose economy seems to be dependent largely on the pearl
trade. In a basic sense, the town depends on the village, for it is the pearl
divers who bring the pearls to the traders. Steinbeck does not really
examine the economic structure of La Paz. However, the main economic
activities mentioned in the novella are fishing and pearl diving, both
performed by the Indians. The other activities described are those performed by the priest, the doctor, and the pearl traders. Of these, both
the priest and the doctor abuse their functions, for they neither comfort
nor heal the poor. The pearl traders too are shown to be exploiting the
Indians, for they have monopolised the market secretly and they do not
pay a fair price.

The whole system is corrupt, with the powerful members of the society
supporting each other to keep the weaker members down. The only
thing which seems to check the power of the traders is their fear of snap-
ping the endurance of the Indians; there is a price below which the pearl
traders dare not go, for it had happened that a fisherman in despair had
given his pearls to the church' (p.22). Steinbeck's criticism emphasises
the deep despair of the Indians, for the church too is not a real refuge.

In describing the exploitative system of La Paz, Steinbeck has condensed the essence of the Spanish conquest of the Indians. Symbolically,
the Indians live in shabby brush houses outside the city walls, as though
denied a place in their community. It is this whole inhuman structure
that compels Kino in anger and frustration to smash his fist against the
doctor's closed gate. As social analysis, *The Pearl* is not very sophisticated: it is not an analytical novel; and Steinbeck is more concerned
with the human dimension of dreaming and suffering.

The characters

The original story of the pearl mentions several characters, none of
whom is developed fully: an Indian boy, a number of girls, some dead

* *The Log from the Sea of Cortez*, Pan Books, London, 1969, pp.161-2.

relatives, a few pearl brokers, a friend, attackers, and pursuers. None of them is given a name. Steinbeck uses all of them in his narrative. Some of them become fully-fledged figures, others are sketched in briefly, and yet others are left deliberately anonymous.

The overall impression is one of a traditional social setting, in which the characters are typical or flat figures, rather than sharply individualised personalities. Steinbeck's characterisation is consistent with the parable-like qualities of *The Pearl*.

The family: Kino, Juana, Coyotito

From the nameless Indian boy of the original tale, Steinbeck created a mature young man, Kino, with a wife and son. It is clear that Steinbeck meant his family to represent an ideal human family: Kino is Man, Juana is Woman, and Coyotito is Child. Juana's reflections on her husband at the beginning of Chapter 5 indicate that Kino as Man and Juana as Woman bear distinctly separate characteristics which make them archetypal figures. They are symbolic of the primal experiences of all mankind.

It is evident, too, that the archetypal, that is, the primitive and universal, characteristics of Kino and Juana make them human, and distinguish them from other biological creatures. To be a man means to be 'half insane and half god' (p.56), for man has spiritual courage and imagination; to be a woman means to preserve life and to endure patiently (p.56).

Kino

Kino's physical appearance is given in broad outline only: brown skin, black hair, thick coarse moustache, and eyes that are warm, fierce, and bright. He is typical of any young and strong man in appearance.

Steinbeck is more concerned with his spiritual qualities. Kino is named after Eusebius Kino, the seventeenth-century Jesuit missionary, who worked among the Gulf Indians. The name signifies goodness, generosity, and courage.

Kino is an illiterate, ignorant fisherman and pearl diver, whose only valuable possession is his canoe. He is simple but not simple-minded. In his simplicity, he cannot always understand or control his emotions, but it is his capacity to feel strong emotion that distinguishes him.

He has a strong and tender relationship with his wife and child, revealed by small incidents: the peaceful silence as Kino eats his breakfast (p.4); when Kino leaves the cave to attack the hunters, he lays his palm on Coyotito's head and touches Juana's cheek in farewell (p.79). The strong family ties extend to his brother, Juan Tomás, as we see from their conversations, and from Juan Tomás's willingness to hide them from the attackers; and even Apolonia's 'formal lament' (p.61) for Kino's 'death' after the fire is a sign of firmly established family ties. Moreover Kino is well liked by his neighbours (p.41), although friendship is weakened by greed for the pearl.

Kino is fierce to protect his family, when their security is threatened: he is husband, father, provider, and protector. He fearlessly destroys the scorpion (p.5); he is ready to fight the predators who skulk around his brush house (p.53); in the desert, his primary concern is to protect his family and he is unhesitatingly ready to sacrifice himself for them (pp.72, 74).

Kino's deeply emotional nature, though, can become passionate and even savage. There are many signs of this: spurned by the doctor, he can only vent his rage by crushing his fist against the locked gate (p.12); when the doctor visits his brush house, Kino feels a smothered rage, hate, and fear (p.29); and he can even hit Juana brutally (p.55). This aspect of his character arises partly from his inarticulateness, his inability to voice the surging emotions within him or to analyse their causes. He is a man of few words. His longest speech is inspired by the visions of the future that he sees in the pearl, and it causes Juana to wonder at his courage and imagination. Kino's complex feelings are buried deeply in him.

He also has a native flair for theatrical effect, which shows itself when bargaining with the pearl traders.

Kino's habitual reticence grows more pronounced after the discovery of the pearl, and develops into a deep sense of loneliness. He becomes cautious and suspicious of everyone. Possession of the pearl sets him apart from the rest of society. In this 'cold and lonely' (p.27) condition, Kino prepares 'a hard skin for himself against the world' (p.28).

Kino's sense of alienation from ordinary life is exacerbated by his concept of religion. Apart from a desire to be married formally in church, Kino does not really think about Christianity. His view of the gods derives from the old religion of his people; and the hostility of the gods towards human endeavour increases his sense of torment.

At the deepest level of Kino's character lies his physical courage and endurance. It is a strength which is channelled into the preservation of himself and his family. He is highly competent in conducting his livelihood. Swimming underwater to search for pearls, Kino feels the pride of physical prowess (p.17). He applies the same deliberate skill and craftsmanship to the care of his canoe (p.14). In the desert Kino's dogged perseverance is a testament of man's great capacity to endure suffering and to survive. Steinbeck traces this human tenacity and determination to the instinctive drive to survive which is found in all living things (p.65).

Juana

Juana's name means 'woman'. She is woman as wife, mother, preserver. Steinbeck's portrayal of Juana is typical of the figure of the earth mother or earth goddess, found in some of his other novels, such as Rama in *To a God Unknown*, and Ma Joad in *The Grapes of Wrath*. Juana is the idealised traditional woman: 'obedient and respectful and cheerful and patient' (p.7), able to endure great physical hardship in silence, and almost as strong as a man. But like Kino, she is also an ignorant and superstitious peasant woman, who can be trapped by the doctor's superior knowledge.

As a wife, she is a perfect helpmate, for she will follow and support Kino in all his undertakings. Although she pleads with him to destroy the pearl, she will not abandon him in time of danger when they are in the desert (p.74). In fact, Kino draws strength from her resolution.

However, it is wrong to think of Juana as merely passive. When she feels that her family is threatened, she is able to judge and make decisions on her own. Thus, watching the troubled Kino after the first attack on him, she concludes that it is best to be free of the pearl (p.37). She continues to plead with Kino to get rid of the pearl, and she even tries to throw it back into the sea herself (p.55).

Juana's actions may best be understood in terms of two major factors which reinforce each other. The first is her role as mother and protector of her family; the second is her concept of womanhood. As a mother, Juana cherishes her son and her family as a whole, and thus will do everything in her power to protect her own.

Juana's concept of a woman is a very traditional one. To her, man is an adventurer: he is driven by his courage and imagination towards ever new goals and dreams, and it is this quality which gives meaning to his existence. But a woman is the complementary half of a man. Her qualities are reason, caution, and the sense of preservation. Juana cannot understand the differences between man and woman, but she accepts them and needs them (p.56).

Juana's strong sense of preservation enables her to protect and keep her family together. Discovering the dead man slain with Kino's knife, she knows at once that she must relinquish the past life, for there is 'nothing to do but to save themselves' (p.57). Steinbeck also seems to suggest that her sense of preservation is instinctive. It arises from that same 'ancient' 'animal thing' (p.65) which enables Kino to lead his family with caution and certainty through the desert. In Steinbeck's description of Juana's physical reaction to danger, there is an echo of this animal or biological drive. The animal part of man (or woman), however, does not necessarily make him any less human. When, with her lips drawn back from her teeth 'like a cat's lips' (p.53), Juana rushes to defend Kino from the dark attackers outside their house, the clearness of her action gives it a certain beauty. Moreover, Kino's and Juana's great love for their child is also an expression of this ancient biological nature of man. Juana's instinct for preservation comes to the fore when it is Coyotito who is in danger. When Coyotito is stung by the scorpion, she immediately attempts to suck out the poison from his wound.

Juana's life probably revolves around Coyotito, for he is her firstborn and 'nearly everything . . . in Juana's world' (p.7). Throughout the novella, her actions show a profound and constant awareness of her son. Coyotito is always by her side, even while she is busy at some task. When she leaves him momentarily, it indicates the terrible urgency of what she must do, such as the time when Kino is attacked and she goes to help him (p.53), or when she leaves the hut furtively to throw the pearl into the sea (p.55). Normally, however, Juana's deep love for her son expresses itself through her singing to him, or her quiet reassuring words, or her playfulness with him, or her desperate prayers in moments of crisis.

The death of Coyotito brings total grief to Juana. It transforms her so completely that it is as though she, too, has been removed from life (p.84).

Coyotito

Coyotito appears quite briefly over many sections of the novella, yet he gradually acquires a special aura of his own. He is the firstborn son and thus symbolic of his parents' hopes for the future. He carries on the family line; he also represents the continuation of life.

When he first appears, he is a beautiful (p.41), happy, and carefree child. He laughs at the dreaded scorpion (p.5), the symbol of evil, because in his innocence he does not yet comprehend the idea of good and evil. This makes him vulnerable to harm.

Coyotito almost dies, twice: firstly, when he is stung by the scorpion; secondly, when the doctor (probably) poisons him. He recovers from both attacks, for he possesses a strong survival drive. He is nature's child, in the sense that the instinct for life and survival is dominant in him.

As his parents go through their suffering, Coyotito seems to grow in awareness. He is not merely passive in the actions of his parents. In fact, he seems to be watching and remembering everything that takes place; and Juana certainly seems to feel that Coyotito has a wordless understanding of his universe (p.42). Coyotito responds appropriately to the emotional states of his parents. He is particularly close to his mother, for she involves him in all that she does: she sings the Song of the Family to him (p.52); she makes sure that Coyotito sees everything when they go to the pearl traders (p.42); and when she takes the pearl out secretly to throw it back into the sea, she pauses to look at Coyotito first (p.55). In his turn, Coyotito looks at his mother, and reassured, sleeps peacefully (p.2), and even after the scorpion's sting, Juana's soft words seem to quieten him (p.9).

The terror overtaking his parents has an imperceptible but profound influence on Coyotito, which he can only voice in his own childlike manner. After the fire burns down Kino's house, Coyotito is terribly frightened (p.60); and he again cries in fear at Kino's bitter identification of the pearl with his soul (p.63).

During the harsh march through the desert, Coyotito finally seems to lose his joyful innocence. Juana says that he 'knows' what is happening, and the baby's solemn face seems to confirm this (p.78).

Coyotito's death seems to be due to malignant chance, since the hunter is only shooting in the general direction of the coyote's cry. However, there is a faint suggestion that there is a link between the coyote and Coyotito, for Coyotito means 'little coyote'. Steinbeck does not explain the death in terms of 'luck', 'the gods', or 'fate'.

THE MINOR CHARACTERS

Of the minor characters, only two are named, Juan Tomás and Apolonia, both members of Kino's family and both sympathetic to Kino. The other characters are deliberately unnamed for two reasons, which depend on their functions in the novella. One group of unnamed characters (the villagers and the beggars) perform the function of the social chorus or background to the story. The other group consists of the evil characters: the doctor, the priest, the pearl traders, the assailants, the trackers and the hunter. These people are nameless in order to intensify the uneasy sense of impersonal evil surrounding Kino and his family. It is as though these unnamed characters represent types of evilness in Kino's world. Indeed the attackers in the night appear to be even more ominous, because they are only identified as 'the dark creeping things' (p.52), a term which reflects the evasive evil of the dark night.

Although the minor characters are types rather than individuals, some of them are portrayed more vividly than others.

The doctor

The doctor is visualised quite fully although he is a flat character,* who does not develop. Steinbeck's portrayal of him tries to suggest the

---

*A type, a two-dimensional character built round a single idea, not individualised.

emotional tensions in his life. He is mercenary, rapacious, cold, and careless with human life. His treatment of the poor fishermen is typical of his race, which has abused and despised the Indians for four centuries. The greed of the doctor is complete, for it is suggested that he might have married his wife for her wealth. The doctor's discontentment seems to show in his fat folds of flesh and the drooping mouth. He longs to return to Paris, where he once kept a mistress, a hard-faced woman whom he has romanticised in his memory. However, the characterisation of the doctor is unsatisfactory because, despite all the psychological details, he is still larger than life and moves with melodramatic actions: for example, it is even hinted that it is the doctor who is the night prowler in Kino's house.

The priest

The priest, like the doctor, also abuses his social position. He misrepresents the attitude of his Church towards the Indian community, using his spiritual authority to keep them in their place, by giving an annual sermon which preaches the sinful consequences of social change. The motivation for the priest's actions is not developed. It is only suggested that he, too, is avaricious although he seems to want the money for repairing church property (p.21).

The pearl buyers

There are many pearl buyers or dealers in La Paz, but they all represent only one man who has total control over the pearl trade. Thus there is no real competition. The four pearl buyers, who are involved in Kino's effort to sell the pearl, are secret conspirators who have worked out an elaborate plan to cheat Kino. The pearl buyers only work for a salary from their patron, but they take pride in driving a hard bargain. Steinbeck seems to suggest that their function as pearl buyers overpowers them, during the excitement of 'the hunt' (p.40).

Four pearl buyers are mentioned, but the first pearl buyer is more sharply portrayed than the others.

The first pearl buyer is a stout man, whose kindly face and sociable manner hide his real nature. What gives him away are his eyes, which look steady and cruel and unwinking as a hawk's eyes when he is evaluating his victim; and his mechanical habit of performing a little trick with a coin. His trick is to roll a coin back and forth with his right hand, making it appear and disappear like magic. It suggests a cunning and dishonesty in the man's real nature. Also, in the moment of stress and excitement, when he first sees Kino's pearl, his hand stumbles, although his face is impassive.

The attackers and the hunters

These anonymous symbols of evil are not characters in the ordinary sense of the word. They perform a literary function: carrying the theme of impersonal evil, to create a sense of inescapable, impending doom.

Steinbeck emphasises their unindividualised character. The men who prowl around Kino's house in the dark are merely 'the dark creeping things' (p.52), and not men. In the desert, another feature of evil appears: the hunter on horseback is helped by two trackers, who are almost animal-like in their ability to track down Kino and his family. Steinbeck uses terms from hunting throughout the episode. He seems to be suggesting, again, that evil is visible in human beings, but that it is inherently a part of the whole natural universe: the hunters are part of the 'black unhuman things' (p.80).

Juan Tomás and Apolonia

Juan Tomás and his wife Apolonia act as foils for Kino and Juana. As the older brother, Juan Tomás is the one from whom Kino seeks advice. Juan Tomás represents traditional society, wise but cautious. He tells Kino that despite their sufferings, their people have always survived. It is a warning to Kino not to be rash, for going into the unknown may be even more dangerous than accepting the known. Kino, in contrast, tells his brother that the outrage he feels is too deep to be accepted passively.

Apolonia is a mere sketch, not a fully drawn character. Only one thing is shown about her, her 'formal lament' (p.61), when she thinks that Kino and his family have been killed in the fire. Her cries are merely the performance of a traditional duty. In contrast, Juana's grief over the death of Coyotito appears to be profoundly moving.

The ideas

In the course of this commentary, it has become evident that *The Pearl* rests on a number of concepts basic to Steinbeck's view of existence as developed in the novella. These basic ideas constitute a framework of reference which helps us to understand the meaning of *The Pearl*; and they can be seen as the abstract structure of the novella. The dominant ideas are the concept of the gods, the concept of 'is-thinking', and the concept of man.

The gods

The religious views of *The Pearl* can be derived mainly from three sources: the priest, Kino, and Juana. Steinbeck's treatment of the priest is satirical. The priest is shown in an unsympathetic light as someone who has debased his religion. Through him, Christianity has become merely a part of the social system to promote the interests of the wealthy and powerful, and to keep the poor and ignorant Indians down. The Church has been corrupted by materialism, for even Masses (prayers for the souls of the dead) can be bought by the rich to ensure their place in heaven (p.10). The only suggestion that the Church was not always so corrupt comes from the fact that Kino was named after a priest who had been a good man.

Christianity is the official religion of La Paz, but it seems to have made little real impact on the Indians, who still have strong emotional connexions with their old religion. Juana's prayers in moments of stress are characteristically made to the old Indian gods, overlaid with the newer Christian prayers. The old Indian religion is buried deep in her mind, as is revealed by her behaviour. After Coyotito is stung by the scorpion, Juana prays that they may find a pearl so as to tempt the doctor to examine the child; she does not pray directly for Coyotito's recovery. Her strange indirection may be explained by analysing the way the Gulf people think about their world.

Steinbeck says that the minds of the Gulf people are 'as unsubstantial as the mirage of the Gulf' (p.15), because things trusted and believed in may turn out to be illusions. The ambiguous nature of their world seems to extend to the Indians' idea of their gods. It was luck to find a pearl, 'a little pat on the back by God or the gods or both' (p.16), but the luck could not really be forced: Juana cannot really 'tear the luck out of the gods' hands' (p.17). In fact, Kino and Juana believe that 'it is not good to want a thing too much . . . You must want it just enough, and you must be very tactful with God or the gods' (p.19). Later, Kino is even more explicit about the gods' attitude to human beings. He believes that 'the gods take their revenge on a man if he be successful through his own efforts' (p.28).

The Indian gods are distant and remote, apparently uncaring about human life. Both Kino and Juana seem to fear their old Indian gods, because the gods are unsympathetic and even malevolent towards human beings. This aspect of Indian religious beliefs indicates the nature of their world, which is almost identifiable with the natural world. The old Indian gods are like those formidable symbols of nature, the sea and the mountain: both capable of inspiring awe, fear, and almost a sense of worship, because of their remote magnificence.

In the beginning of the novella, Steinbeck draws an image of the Indian world: a symbolic image of the indifference of the gods, and of the affinity between human and natural existence; and suggesting that existence is brutal and even fatalistic. Looking around at the stirring signs of life in the early dawn, Kino observes the excited behaviour of an ant in the dust: 'Kino watched with the detachment of God while a dusty ant frantically tried to escape the sand trap an ant lion had dug for him' (p.2).

Steinbeck's 'ant' symbol of life suggests that the universe operates under impersonal forces. The 'ant' symbol may be interpreted in two ways, either philosophically or scientifically. Scientifically, the symbol may be analysed further in the context of Steinbeck's non-teleological ideas (which will be discussed in the next section: see 'Is-thinking'). Philosophically, the 'ant' symbol may be interpreted by seeing the forces which operate in the universe as 'the gods'. The symbol offers an explanation of the nature of evil in the novella.

There is a pervasive sense of the impersonality of evil in the universe of *The Pearl*. From the very beginning, Kino's apprehension of evil comes in the form of the music of evil which he hears in moments of danger. The Song of Evil simply arises, as, for example, it comes when the baby falls sick after the doctor's treatment (p.33). Reinforcing the significance of the Song of Evil is the sense of a diffuse evilness spread all around. Kino and Juana often refer to their fear of 'the evils of the night' (p.66), so that the family seems embattled on all sides. Finally, even the agents of evil are nameless. As such, they are anonymous and impersonal, merely 'the dark creeping things' (p.52), merely the embodiment of 'the evil' (p.52) that is in the universe.

The universal and impersonal nature of evil in the novella strongly suggests the fatalism of Kino's world. Despite his courage and persistence, Kino easily feels depressed by events; and it is only Juana's consistency and encouragement which enable him to continue. When Kino does not get a fair price from the pearl dealers, he is almost overwhelmed by a feeling of the inevitability of failure. Steinbeck describes this in language which stresses the helplessness of the individual against such a miasma of evil, but as a tool of analysis, such language appears to be sentimental and imprecise. Steinbeck has become Kino in this situation so that his sympathy swamps everything else, as he makes Kino in the pearl dealer's office feel:

> the creeping of fate, the circling of wolves, the hover of vultures. He [feels] the evil coagulating about him, and he [is] helpless to protect himself. He [hears] in his ears the evil music (p.48).

The failure of language in the above passage indicates a more strenuous flaw in the nature of *The Pearl*'s vision. The weakness in Steinbeck's analysis of Kino's, and thus of man's, predicament—for Kino represents man—lies in the inability of non-teleological thinking to explain adequately the problems of good and evil in *The Pearl*.

'Is-thinking'

In *The Log from the Sea of Cortez*, Steinbeck discusses the notion of non-teleological thinking, which he essentially defines as seeing things as they are, rather than seeing things in terms of why they are. Teleology is the study of final causes in things, so as to discover their purpose; thus non-teleology sees things in themselves, and asserts that 'a thing is because it is'. From this line of reasoning, non-teleological thinking became known as 'is-thinking'.

It is evident that *The Pearl* demonstrates some of the effects of 'is-thinking': the impersonal sense of evil which Kino feels, the Song of Evil which sounds in his mind, seem to arise spontaneously in his world. However, it would be dangerous to generalise the applicability of ideas from *The Log from the Sea of Cortez* to *The Pearl*. *The Log from the Sea of Cortez*, after all, was not completely the product of Steinbeck's efforts. The book was produced jointly by Steinbeck and Ricketts, and some of its views are not consistent with Steinbeck's other published works. A striking and relevant example of this kind of contradiction can be seen by comparing *The Log from the Sea of Cortez* with *The Forgotten Village*. *The Log from the Sea of Cortez* regards social change and progress as signs of degeneration in the human species; but *The Forgotten Village* advocates the introduction of modern medicine to fight disease in a small traditional Mexican village (rather like Kino's Indian village).

However, Steinbeck was attracted to some aspects of 'is-thinking', particularly the ease with which 'is-thinking' could adapt itself to an ecological view of life. By looking at life as it 'is', Steinbeck believed that he would be able to perceive the mutual relations between individual organisms (including man) and their environment. He thought that the universe was a whole; and the study of the inner relationships within the whole would lead to greater understanding of the holistic basis of life (the tendency of life to strive towards wholeness). In *The Log from the Sea of Cortez*, Steinbeck calls the holistic tendency of life a 'religious' feeling.

> And it is a strange thing that most of the feeling we call religious, most of the mystical outcrying which is one of the most prized and used and desired reactions of our species, is really the understanding and the attempt to say that man is related to the whole thing, related inextricably to all reality, known and unknowable.*

Religion is 'the attempt to say that man is related to the whole thing': in these words, Steinbeck has defined the philosophical basis of *The Pearl*. The image of Kino looking impassively at the dusty ant struggling

* Steinbeck, *The Log from the Sea of Cortez*, Pan Books, London, 1969, p.267.

in the trap of the ant lion is not the final picture of life. The scientific objectivity which such a view implies is indeed the result of 'is-thinking', but Steinbeck's philosophical detachment is qualified by a religious impulse. The natural world inevitably leads man towards the celebration of a higher principle of cosmic order, of universal concord: man transcends the bare objectivity of things to discover the harmony of all things. In the rather simple symbolism of the ant, man may seem to be pitted against the cruelty of fate (or the gods) in a universe which seems to have no meaning, but man's struggles do have a pattern within the holistic structure of life, within the view of the whole of life. Thus, the dusty ant reappears in the desert to parallel Kino's flight: 'he watched the ants moving, a little column of them near to his foot, and he put his foot in their path. Then the column climbed over his instep and continued on its way, and Kino left his foot there and watched them move over it' (p.67).

Steinbeck's view that life strives towards the harmony of the whole is not unique to his thinking. It is a basic element in many Eastern philosophies, and Steinbeck may possibly have been influenced by his knowledge of some Sanskrit poetry. A more immediate and discernable source of influence is that of American Transcendentalism. This was a school of philosophy in the nineteenth century, whose leaders were Emerson (1803–82) and Thoreau (1817–62). Their ideas included the unity of all things, and the need to transcend physical sensory knowledge through the truth of intuition.

Both these ideas play a part in *The Pearl*, for ultimately *The Pearl* is a philosophical (or 'religious' in Steinbeck's sense) work. It defines a vision of life in which man is but a small and inextricable part of a greater whole of the universe; and man's attempt to understand his place in that universe is a religious striving to discover the meaning of life.

Man

Man in *The Pearl* is very much a social animal. He is part of a social structure which both exploits him and sustains him; and he is also part of a family structure which helps to define his being.

As a fisherman and pearl diver, Kino has a certain function in his community. The image of the town itself suggests his role in the community. The town is called 'a colonial animal' (p.21). This suggests a system of organisation in which all the individual organisms have cooperated to form the appearance of a single combined unit. It suggests a high degree of interdependency within the system. Kino is part of a link that extends from the pearl divers to the pearl dealers, cloth merchants, beggars, doctor, and priest. In this sense, the pearl merely crystallises the submerged relationships. The biological terminology suggests that the system of interdependency itself is not an evil thing. Like a growing coral, the 'colonial' organisation helps to make the town self-sufficient and self-defensive.

From a certain point of view, such as that of economics, Kino is the victim. However, it is necessary to qualify this view. Juan Tomás reminds him that they have always managed to survive within the system. More significantly, Kino himself feels the terror of being outside the system. After the priest's visit, Kino reflects that he has 'broken through the horizons into a cold and lonely outside' (p.27), and it makes him feel 'alone and unprotected' (p.27).

What sustains Kino in his sense of alienation, of estrangement, of being cut off from his surroundings, is his family: he is not totally cast out and alone. He is also sustained, indeed driven forward, by another source of strength. This is his inner courage and imagination. Steinbeck tells us quite directly that it is this unique aspect of man's nature which separates him from the rest of the biological universe, for 'it is one of the greatest talents the species [man] has and one that has made it superior to animals that are satisfied with what they have' (p.24).

The idea of man's unique 'imagination' (p.24) is developed further by Juana's thoughts on the subject. She sees this ability to imagine, to desire the unknown and to conquer it, as the one thing that distinguishes a man from a woman, and makes him strong. What matters is not that the man should win in his struggle, but that he should make the attempt to the utmost of his capability.

In the universe of *The Pearl*, man's effort—his fight against 'the mountain' and 'the sea' (p.56)—seems doomed to certain destruction. Man, despite his courage, determination, and perseverance, seems too weak and puny to fight against the order of things. Juan Tomás warns Kino about defying 'the whole structure, the whole way of life' (p.51). The significance of his words is enlarged by the philosophical framework of *The Pearl*, to include Steinbeck's vision of the very nature of existence.

Steinbeck's philosophy: some conclusions

Steinbeck's philosophy in *The Pearl* seems to contain an inherent ambiguity. Seen as a moral parable about materialistic greed, *The Pearl* contains characterisations of people perverted by greed: the doctor, the priest, and the pearl buyers, in particular. These people are immoral or evil in that they personally try to defraud Kino.

However, stylistically, *The Pearl* suggests an alternative meaning based on the significance of the subject matter. Throughout the novella, these evil men are juxtaposed with images of 'slaughter' (p.32) in nature:

hungry dogs and pigs scavenge for dead animals on the beach (p.13); in the sea bottom life and death are an endless cycle (p.13); big fishes eat little fishes, and night hawks hunt night mice (p.32); in the mountain pool wild animals drink 'water through their bloody teeth' (p.76); and even the great pearl is torn out of 'dying flesh' (p. 19). The images combine thematically to suggest that 'slaughter', from the perspective of nature, is just the inevitable process of living and dying. It is not really a 'moral' event. La Paz is only another great tide pool or sea bottom, in which different kinds of men live and kill each other in order to go on living.

It is clear that such a conclusion is distasteful to Steinbeck in *The Pearl*. He emphasises the repulsive qualities of the doctor and the priest, so that they seem to be personally repugnant. Also, Steinbeck takes some pains to suggest that the history of conquest in Mexico was a history of inhuman repression. For example, the doctor is 'of a race which for nearly four hundred years had beaten and starved and robbed and despised Kino's race' (p.9).

Steinbeck is too much of a humanist to view human suffering dispassionately, with the coldly detached eye of the scientist looking through his microscope at micro-organisms killing each other. *The Pearl* is above all a moving testament to human suffering. As such, it suggests the moral anger of *The Grapes of Wrath*.

Steinbeck's humanitarianism, his concern for human grief and anguish, can be traced to the sense of hopelessness that pervades *The Pearl*. The novella has an intense 'outrage' (p.52) at its centre, against the implacability of fate. After all, Juana's image is the correct one: man with all his courage 'would drive his strength against a mountain and plunge his strength against the sea' (p.56), but ultimately the mountain and the sea would remain fixed and immovable. The real sea and mountain in *The Pearl*, in fact, are seen as things that will endure, and that will remain unmoved and unchanged by all man's efforts. They are quite indifferent to human life: they simply 'are'—to use the language of Steinbeck's philosophy.

It is Juana's old Indian religion that comes closest to expressing this view of cosmic implacability, of a world in which forces beyond man's understanding or control are completely unrelenting towards man. Juana's behaviour demonstrates the old Indian concept of the gods, that is, of the forces which control her world. Chance and luck seem to dominate this world. The gods are even more hostile in Kino's view: he believes that the gods will punish man for attempting to change his life, for pitting his strength against the mountain.

In the end, Kino and Juana have learned wisdom. They seem to have looked into the secret meaning of life, but their knowledge sets them apart. They become 'remote' (p.84) and 'immune' (p.85), removed from ordinary existence. It is as though their knowledge cannot be expressed, cannot be communicated. Thus at the heart of *The Pearl* there is a deep silence, the silence of pain and the silence of knowledge.

Style and meaning

A retold tale

The Pearl has made an accurate study of the customs, beliefs, language, and tensions in the way of life of a Mexican community. It offers a concrete picture of this community by means of realistic detailed description of the way Kino and his neighbours live: the appearance of their brush houses, the food they eat, the clothes they wear, their canoes, how they dive for pearls, their religious beliefs. To a lesser degree, *The Pearl* also contains a study of the townspeople in this community, with brief sketches of some of its leading citizens. However accurate or realistic some of its details may be though, *The Pearl* is fiction. The novella cannot reproduce the exact words and actions of the people being observed: such a method would make it a technical report rather than a work of art. Steinbeck's La Paz on the Gulf is an emotionally sharpened picture. The dialogue takes on the rhythms of life shaped by art; the gestures of people, the events of the story are chosen for the insights they give into the characters of people or the nature of their existence. Steinbeck's style here is a blend of 'life' and 'art'. His method may be compared with the image of the Gulf in the novella: 'the uncertain air' of the mirage that 'magnified some things and blotted out others . . . so that all sights were unreal and vision could not be trusted; so that sea and land had the sharp clarities and the vagueness of a dream' (pp.13–14).

The Pearl's mirage or dreamlike quality is condensed in the image of the pearl itself. Its appearance suggests both loveliness and illusion: 'the great pearl, perfect as the moon . . . captured the light and refined it and gave it back in silver incandescence' (p. 19). Significantly, Kino is at first reluctant to open the oyster. He is aware that in the uncertain world of the Gulf, there are 'more illusions than realities' (p.19). Then in the surface of the pearl, he sees 'dream forms' (p.19). Steinbeck's style here is not just descriptive: he is not just describing the shape and feel of the pearl; he is suggesting the thematic meaning of the pearl. His style is functional, being completely fused with the content of the book.

The Pearl's dreamlike quality is combined with its simplicity. Steinbeck has retained the starkness of parable (a simple story with a parallel moral meaning) so that *The Pearl* seems to be composed from elemental units of meaning. These basic elements of life can be expressed thus:

man, woman, and child; sea, beach, desert, and mountain; man, nature, and the gods; good and evil. In his introduction to *The Pearl*, Steinbeck himself calls attention to this aspect of his novella: 'as with all retold tales that are in people's hearts, there are only good and bad things and black and white things and good and evil things, and no in-between anywhere'. It is in the nature of such a retold tale to deal with those archetypal elements, which are enumerated above, for those basic elements are formed from the primitive experiences of all mankind.

It is also in the nature of a retold tale to have a narrative framework, as though the story is seen in the perspective of time. Steinbeck achieves this effect of a timeless legend in *The Pearl* by firstly, having the introductory lines at the beginning of the novella, which make the tale a parable: the opening words, 'In the town they tell the story of . . .', are similar to the magical formula of timeless children's stories, 'Once upon a time . . .' Secondly, Steinbeck repeats this motif at the end, so that the return of the family to La Paz is seen as an event in the memory of the old men. He makes the story universal, a story of Everyman: 'it is an event that happened to everyone' (p.84). Thus the story of *The Pearl* is framed by the narrative device of retelling it in the race memory of man.

The features of dream and parable give *The Pearl* a lyrical quality, which Steinbeck described as a heightened atmosphere that all folkstories have. The lyrical atmosphere raises the folk-story above the level of ordinary and prosaic events in actual life, so that everything appears slightly larger than life. The story and the characters appear to be simplified, and they achieve a degree of clarity of meaning seldom found in real life. This is probably what Steinbeck means by saying that there are 'only good and bad things and black and white things and good and evil things and no in-between anywhere'. Another feature of the lyricism is that the narrative is told in a slightly bardic tone, as though being chanted by the traditional village poet-singer, who told tales of heroic endeavour in the collective history of the race.

The lyricism of *The Pearl* is enhanced by a number of stylistic features, including the use of songs, the rhythmic quality of its language, the blend of imagery into a distinctive pattern, and finally that fleeting quality of illusion in *The Pearl* which gives it a dreamlike aura.

The songs

The songs are the heritage of the local people: only Kino's people have songs, the townspeople do not have such a tradition. The Gulf people were once 'great makers of songs' (p.1), suggesting that they had once been a richly creative people with a culture of their own, before the Spanish conquest of their land. The songs of the Gulf people represent their vision, their interpretation of their lives, for they had made songs

of 'everything they saw or thought or did or heard' (p.1); they 'had sung
of everything that happened or existed' (p.16).

Like the canoes, these songs are passed on from generation to
generation: they are a link to the past history of the Gulf people. In one
sense the songs can never be destroyed, even if some of them may be
forgotten eventually, for the songs have been absorbed into the racial
memory, or generic memory, of the Gulf people. Thus all the songs,
including 'the ones forgotten' (p.16), are in Kino and his people.

The songs give a dimension of depth to the characterisation of Kino
and Juana. Part of their nature derives from the shared past of their
people. They seem to embody the strength of this past in their moral
fortitude. Kino, in particular, seems to be a sensitive conduit between
the past and the present, so that he alone seems to hear the songs from
the tradition of the Gulf people, although it is not very certain whether
he alone listened to the songs, or whether all of his people did it (p.1).
Juana sings one of the songs, the Song of the Family, from time to time.

The songs mean various things. The Song of the Family is a good
song, which comes from the sound of waves breaking rhythmically on
the beach, the comfortable sounds of Juana's daily household tasks. It
is a song which celebrates the familiar way of life of the family. When
Juana sings it, the Song of the Family proclaims the safety, the warmth,
the sanctity of the family (p.3), linking the family to the wholeness and
harmony of life.

The Song of the Enemy, or the Song of Evil, is the music of 'any foe
of the family' and it has 'a savage, secret, dangerous melody' (p.4). It is
associated with the scorpion (p.4), the priest (p.26), the doctor after he
poisons Coyotito (p.33), the night intruders (pp.36,52), the pearl dealers
who try to cheat Kino (p.48), the broken canoe (p.59), the hunter and
the trackers (p.73). The music of evil is also associated with the pearl,
after its dream forms become sinister (pp.68,86). The music of evil is
self-explanatory, for it merely underscores the theme of evil; it emphasises those moments of danger to the family which threaten to
destroy its existence.

There are minor songs, like the Song of the Undersea, which Kino
hears while searching for oysters in the waters of the Gulf. But the third
major song is the Song of the Pearl, which first appears very faintly as
the Song of the Pearl That Might Be, 'a secret little inner song, hardly
perceptible . . . sweet and secret and clinging' (p.17), because Kino is
longing to find a pearl for Coyotito's sake. The music of the pearl swells
out with the actual discovery of the great pearl, so that the initial secret
little melody becomes 'glowing and gloating and triumphant' (p.19).
The Song of the Pearl is beautiful because of its promise of a new life
for the family. Thus in Kino's mind, the music of the pearl mingles with
the music of the family.

Stylistically, the songs perform two major functions. The first appearance of each song announces a fresh thematic development. Thus, the Song of the Family introduces the theme of the family on that first morning with which the novella opens, and subsequent developments are emphasised at appropriate stages by recalling the thematic music of the family; and a similar process occurs with the other two main songs. The songs may also combine to suggest the intertwining of the themes: such as when the Song of the Pearl merges with the Song of the Family, as Kino reads the future in the shapes on the pearl's surface (p.23); or when the Song of the Family is contrasted to the music of evil, because Coyotito is ill from the doctor's white powder (p.33).

The second main function of the songs is to weave a distinctive pattern out of the events of the story. Since the songs carry the theme of *The Pearl*, they may be seen as the musical equivalent of the ideas of the novella. The songs form a musical or rhythmic pattern that follows the thematic pattern closely, so that the music helps to unite the separate strands of the story. This musical pattern is part of the structure of *The Pearl*.

Steinbeck's treatment of the songs is rather reminiscent of cinematic techniques. In film, music is often used in combination with the visual image, and this is precisely the technique of *The Pearl*.

Cinematic influence

The Pearl makes use of a number of techniques normally associated with film. This is hardly surprising as Steinbeck was involved with the film production of many of his novels in the 1940s; and in fact *The Pearl* was filmed in 1948.

Visually, *The Pearl* has a sustained photographic clarity of detail, which is very evident in the sharpness of its physical description: the plain brush houses; the bare, clean interior of Kino's hut; the stone and plaster houses of the town, with its blinding plaza (or square) and church; the doctor's gloomy, heavily furnished room, with its delicate china and silver; the Spanish-style houses, with their harsh sun-drenched outer walls but cool inner gardens; the pearl buyers' offices with barred windows. The vividness of Steinbeck's physical scenes extends to the natural landscape: the beach of yellow sand with its line of shell and algae; the rich profusion of life on the sea bottom; the hot dry feel of the desert; and the mountain cleft with its little stony pools of water. The physical sense of *The Pearl*'s world is very keen, helping to root the parable firmly to the real earth, and this physical acuity is typical of Steinbeck's strength as a novelist. However, the physical vividness is not identical with photographic realism, for over everything is the uncertain air, the brooding, elusive atmosphere of the Gulf mirage.

Another cinematic quality of *The Pearl* is the sound-track (as it is called in film) which accompanies the action. The songs constitute the most important part of the sound effects, but scattered throughout the novella are other thematic sounds. These are the sounds emitted by animals, birds, and fishes: in the early dawn of the first day, there are the familiar sounds of roosters crowing, little birds chittering; as the doctor feeds on chocolate and sweet cakes, there are the sounds of 'slaughter' (p.32) in the estuary; when the family flees into the desert, they are accompanied by the sounds of coyotes crying, owls screeching, the undergrowth crackling. These subsidiary animal sounds serve as a refrain or a chorus to remind us of the closeness of nature, and the affinity to nature, of human existence.

However, as a novelistic technique it is doubtful whether a sound-track is really effective. The minor sounds made by the animals are unobtrusive, on the whole, and as such probably work as part of the overall picture of *The Pearl*. The songs, on the other hand, intrude upon the narrative rather ostentatiously: they call attention to themselves, and as such become decorative devices.

There is a third kind of cinematic technique used in *The Pearl*. To continue with the terminology of film, this may be called the lighting effects. *The Pearl* possesses a quality of light which derives from the illusory, uncertain air of the Gulf, and from the luminous glow of the pearl. The whole narrative seems to be immersed in an atmosphere which is mysterious, illusory, and magical. Because this aura is suggested through the richly evocative images of the Gulf and the pearl, it possesses a potent, haunting quality which is quite effective: unlike the obtrusive device of the thematic music.

The atmospheric lighting of *The Pearl* is modified by another sort of lighting effect. This is the effect derived from a series of images describing light and darkness, which infiltrate the whole novella. The imagery of light and darkness is discussed in the next section of these Notes.

Imagery

An image is a vivid, mental word picture, or a metaphor, which helps to convey an idea. Taken collectively, the images of a literary work can suggest the overall tonality and even the overall significance of the literary work. Groups of images may occur, which deal with a common subject. To consider such clusters of images, called thematic imagery, can help us to analyse a text critically.

Two main image clusters occur in *The Pearl*. They are, firstly, the images dealing with light and darkness, and, secondly, the images dealing with the pool of life.

The thematic imagery of light and darkness in *The Pearl* weaves a fine textural pattern over the whole novella, with the imagery occurring as details which are sometimes almost submerged in the background. The images centre upon the idea of light, darkness, night, and shadow.

The basic pattern of the imagery of light, shadow, and darkness is formed by the cycle of day and night. The narrative events take place over five days, but the narrative opens with early dawn and closes with late dusk. Kino awakens 'in the near dark' (p.1) before dawn, with the eastern sky just becoming brighter. When he throws the pearl back into the sea, the sun is beginning to set, and the darkness of night is approaching. The cycle of day and night reflects the thematic development of Kino's life. He travels from the difficult but endurable, and even beautiful, condition of life of a poor fisherman to the condition of deep, irretrievable loss, and even despair, of having 'gone through pain and . . . come out on the other side' (p.85). The early dawn is of hope, and the dusk is of moral despair.

Throughout the novella, night is associated with darkness and evil. The agents of evil come to attack in the dark night; they are creatures of darkness themselves, being 'black unhuman things' (p.80).

Conversely, day is associated with light and brightness. However, the quality of light is extremely ambiguous, despite the fact that Steinbeck disarmingly acknowledges 'no in-between' things anywhere. The Gulf light is disconcertingly dubious, revealing illusions rather than reality. Moreover, the light may be treacherous: the scorpion basks in a golden shaft of sunlight before it attacks. It is as though light (and thus its moral equivalent, good) generates its own darkness, or at least, carries with it the complementary quality of shadow. Steinbeck has flooded the world of *The Pearl* with a strong, almost blinding, sunshine, so that every person and every object casts a little shadow. This image of the twin-like nature of light and shadow comes out dominantly in the opening scenes: when the procession of people march into town to seek the doctor, the yellow sun throws 'their black shadows ahead of them so that they [walk] on their own shadows' (p.8); at the doctor's closed gate, again 'the glaring sun [throws] the bunched shadows of the people blackly on the white wall' (p.10). The ambiguity extends to inanimate objects, for 'even tiny stones [throw] shadows on the ground' (p.44). Light is qualified by its companion shadow. The two seem inseparable. This imagery of light and shadow suggests that darkness (the shadow cast by evil) is an integral part of existence, giving a sombre tone to *The Pearl*.

The second major image cluster concerns the pool of life. There are three distinct references to this image: the 'sea bottom' in Chapter 2 (p.13); the 'estuary' in Chapter 3 (p.32); and the mountain 'pools' in Chapter 6 (pp.75–6). Taken together, this group of images suggests a microcosmic picture of life, a small self-contained world which mirrors the larger universe as a whole, including the world of man.

The sea bottom image introduces the idea that life is prolific, 'rich with crawling and swimming and growing things' (p.13). The sea bottom image is extended to include the beach, where hungry dogs and pigs from the town scavenge ceaselessly for 'any dead fish or sea bird' (p.13). Even death is incorporated into the cycle of natural regeneration through the dogs and pigs which represent the lowest denomination in the world.

The idea of death being a part of the process is developed further in the estuary image. In the river mouth, the 'slaughter' (p.32) of little fishes by big fishes seems to be inevitable and necessary for the continuation of life. On land, too, the killing is carried out as night hawks hunt night mice. The image of the killing of the smaller by the greater is placed in conjunction with the image of the fat, powerful doctor dining on rich food; and the whole is placed in the context of the doctor preying on the fears of the weak, helpless Kino and Juana (p.29). The parallel between man and nature forces a conclusion of the inevitability of the hunt (these words become literally true when the family is hunted like animals in the desert). This conclusion seems to be as far as Steinbeck wants to go. The repugnant doctor seems to invite intense personal dislike, unlike the big fishes or night hawks, hunting merely for survival.

In the final image, the idea of killing and death is incorporated totally into the cycle of nature. In the lovely, peaceful cleft of the mountain, the pools of water seem almost idyllic. They are a source of life; animals come to drink. Somewhat melodramatically, Steinbeck calls them 'places of killing' (p.76) too, a source of death because animals also kill their prey in these environs.

The main strands of thematic imagery suggest the continuity between human life and biological life, and the presence of animal imagery in general tends to support such an interpretation. However, Steinbeck's biological view of life is modified by his vision of the unique nature of human existence (see the section on Steinbeck's ideas in these Notes (pp.47–54).

There are some images in *The Pearl* which achieve such an intensity of suggestion and meaning that they are really symbols. And the central symbol is of course the great pearl, though there are others such as the canoe, the rifle, Kino's house, and the journey across the desert which should be considered too.

The pearl's appearance has been discussed already (see The nature of *The Pearl*, pp.35–6). Its loveliness seems to be an illusion to draw men on to dream. As such, the pearl serves to elicit the best aspects of human imagination. Gazing into its beauty, Kino dreams of breaking away from the limitations of the old life. The changes made by Steinbeck to the original story are significant, for they reveal the dignity and grandeur of Kino's dreams for his son: the pearl is to bring not just material goods but also love, understanding, and wisdom (p.25). As realisation of the evils brought by possession of the pearl comes upon Kino, he begins to see nightmarish forms instead in the pearl (pp.67–8). Finally, just before he flings the pearl back into the sea, he sees the distorted ugliness that the pearl has become (p.86). The transmutations of the pearl do not indicate that the pearl is inherently evil. It seems simply to reflect and to expose human desires and fears: it shows what is already in men's minds. As such, the pearl is a catalyst, starting off a chain reaction of good or evil in human beings. As the pearl settles into the sea bottom, at the end, it is again lovely, awaiting a new hand to find it and thus start the cycle of dream, distortion, reality, and evil all over again.

Kino's house and canoe represent the stability of tradition in his present life. The house is sanctuary, the dwelling of his family. Its invasion by the night intruder suggests that nothing is safe or sacred, for evil infiltrates everything. The canoe (see the section on *The Pearl* as a social document, pp.36–40) is a spiritual bond to the past of his people. The destruction of the canoe and the house comes at a time when the old way of life has been completely destroyed, for Kino as a murderer is an outcast from his society.

The rifle seems to symbolise the world beyond the reach of the fishermen, for when Kino expresses a wish to own a rifle, his neighbours are amazed by his wild imagination. It may suggest the world of power, for the Spanish conquerors had come with 'gunpowder' (p.43) to back up their authority, and thus the rifle is also an instrument of death. It is this meaning which Kino discovers in the end. Ironically, the rifle is the only dream fulfilled by the pearl, for when Kino returns to La Paz he carries the rifle which has killed his son and, at the same time, all his hope.

The journey across the desert made by Kino and his family is a physical test of the family's endurance and ability to survive. It brings to mind the western journey across the desert in *The Grapes of Wrath*, which, performed on a vast scale, was an exodus, a migration or departure, of people seeking the promised land;* an idea which is probably influenced by the Bible. The desert journey in *The Pearl* has a similar significance, for the family is also seeking the promised land (the capital, where they will sell the pearl and so achieve their dreams). The idea of a spiritual goal is borne out further, because the journey becomes a kind of pilgrimage, in the course of which the moral understanding of the pilgrim is not only tested, but strengthened, and deepened.

---

*The Book of Exodus in the Bible describes the departure of the Israelites out of Egypt in search of the Land of Canaan, promised to Abraham; hence promised land means paradise or any place of happiness.

The language

The Pearl is written in a mixture of styles, which are not always fused together. Some of the language is so emotionally charged that it appears sentimental and rhetorical. The awkward effect is brought out by the simplification of emotion, as, for instance, when Kino refuses the offer of the first pearl dealer:

> Kino had grown tight and hard. He felt the creeping of fate, the circling of wolves, the hover of vultures. He felt the evil coagulating about him, and he was helpless to protect himself. He heard in his ears the evil music. (p.48)

However, such flowery and imprecise language is rare in *The Pearl*. But the danger of slipping into emotionalism is always present, because *The Pearl* is, after all, a rather melodramatic tale, with people whose actions are made up of large, simple gestures. Indeed, Steinbeck's achievement can be seen in the way he has deepened the meaning of the Indian folk-tale. Part of this achievement is due to the hard clarity of the prose description of the setting, the physical actions, and the vivid sketches of people in their homes.

It would also be a mistake to think of the realistic language as being better than the lyrical and emotional language (even if such an arbitrary division were possible). Part of *The Pearl*'s strength also comes from the poetic evocativeness of its language, such as the description of the Gulf air, or the pearl itself.

The 'point of view'

The narrative is told in the form of a 'retold tale', as Steinbeck calls it in his introduction to *The Pearl*. Although there is no personified narrator, there may be felt the directing mind of the omniscient narrator. The ominiscient narrator, or the all-knowing narrator, presumably speaks for Steinbeck himself. He reads the minds of all the characters and reveals their secret thoughts. He interprets the action, and makes moral judgements explicitly. The whole narrative is viewed through the interpreting consciousness of the omniscient narrator (author). In many places, Steinbeck intrudes into the narrative in order to describe the meaning of his story, for example where he analyses the ecology of a town, comparing it to an organism and discussing how news travels in such a system (pp.21,39); or when he analyses the poisonous effects of Kino's possession of the pearl upon the town (pp.22-3).

Steinbeck also uses the minor characters indirectly to suggest his view. The beggars fulfil this role well, since they are detached observers of the scene. For example, they view Kino and Juana critically during the visit to the doctor's house, and conclude, cynically but correctly, that the doctor will not be impressed by their financial status (p.8). Through the beggars, Steinbeck also analyses the faults of the doctor (p.9).

Structure and unity

The structure of a novel is essentially the organisation of its materials; the way in which the different components are put together to become one. The organisation of materials in *The Pearl* can be seen in terms of the story, or the ideas, or the structural devices such as the songs and the imagery. All these elements combine to make a unified work.

The events of the story is the simplest level of organisation, depending on the movement of the action. The story of Kino and Juana is the central action, around which the other events take place, against the background of a physical landscape which forms an appropriate setting for each stage of the action.

The physical landscape has a significant place in the structure of the novella. As the action develops, the scene changes to reflect the nature of the events taking place. The organising principle of the landscape may be formulated in the following way:

THE BEACH (Chapters 1–3) including the village and the sea: introduction to the fishermen's way of life (both its simplicity and the danger it faces, seen in the scorpion and the pearl);

THE TOWN (Chapters 4–5): plot complications (including the pearl buyers and the attackers);

THE DESERT (Chapter 6) including the mountain and the cave: crisis of flight, death, and eventual resolution (the return).

The novella can also be seen as a symphonic arrangement, a view which is encouraged by the presence of its music. The major subjects or themes are accompanied by the appropriate music. Steinbeck was interested in composing a novel on the basis of a musical arrangement. He has said, for instance, that *Cannery Row* reflects the music of Bach in its complicated arrangement of parts.

The theme

The strength of *The Pearl* seems to come from its combination of realism with some other more elusive quality, that element which Steinbeck calls the parable nature of his novella. *The Pearl* has a simplicity which is suggestive of richly symbolic meaning in its very starkness; and the lyrical intensity of some of its language lends itself to thematic interpretation.

The story of Kino is the story of Everyman. More particularly, it is the story of man's search for his soul, in the course of which he encounters good and evil. Seen in this way, *The Pearl* is not very different from its sources (the Indian legend, 'The Hymn of the Soul' of Judas Thomas, and the parable of the pearl in Matthew 13:45-6). However, Steinbeck has deepened the human dimension of his theme, so that the search becomes a humanising process as well as a journey through knowledge of good and evil.

As the narrative opens, Kino and Juana live the almost mindless contentment of unthinking humanity. Their world does have the simplicity of parable, in which all things are either good or bad with no in-between anywhere. The family is good, the enemy is bad: these are almost instinctive responses.

The educative or humanising process begins as soon as the enemy is encountered. The scorpion introduces them to the idea of evil, which possession of the pearl will enlarge in their lives. Significantly, the poison of the pearl is likened to 'the black distillate [of] the scorpion' (p.23). As the moral education of Kino and Juana continues, their characters develop. Kino learns about loneliness, hate, suspicion, and the many forms of evil, including that within himself (he strikes his wife; he begins to perceive that he must hate his own people; he becomes a murderer). Slowly he realises the intricacy of the relationship of evil to the whole, as the beautiful pearl becomes more ambiguous in its power of illusion. But the crisis of consciousness, the complete initiation into evil, only comes at the cave in the mountain. As he crawls out of the womblike cave, Kino is to be spiritually reborn, and the price for this moment of moral awareness is the sacrifice of his firstborn.

At the conclusion of the narrative, Kino has looked full into life, and has seen the horror that may lie at the centre of existence. He has, thus, achieved full human consciousness, full knowledge of the range of human possibility. In this sense, *The Pearl* is a parable based on the Fall of man in the Book of Genesis.

However, *The Pearl*'s definition of man does not end with consciousness. Kino and Juana (who has accompanied him on this pilgrimage) return to the city completely transformed: they are removed, distant, and immune. Their knowledge has alienated them utterly from ordinary existence. Their moral stance suggests the words from T.S. Eliot's poem 'Burnt Norton' (1935), one of his *Four Quartets*: 'human kind/Cannot bear very much reality'. It is as though Steinbeck believes that, in the process of becoming aware of the good and evil bounds of human life, man loses his ordinary humanity, and becomes wise but like the angels of God.

Part 4

Hints for study

The plot

The Pearl has no chapter headings, but these suggested headings may help us to remember the main theme of each chapter.

Brief synopsis

Chapter 1: The scorpion sting
The day begins beautifully for Kino the fisherman and his wife, Juana. Then their baby, Coyotito, is stung by a scorpion. They take the baby to the doctor in town, but leave in frustration as the doctor refuses to treat the child.

Chapter 2: The pearl
Kino dives for pearl oysters in the Gulf and finds a great pearl.

Chapter 3: The false dreams of the pearl
The whole town of La Paz knows that Kino has found the Pearl of the World. The priest and doctor both pay visits to Kino. That night, Kino is attacked. He is not hurt and the pearl is safe.

Chapter 4: The pearl buyers
Kino tries to sell his pearl to the dealers in La Paz. They offer him a ridiculously low price and he decides to sell his pearl in the capital instead. In the night, Kino is attacked again.

Chapter 5: The old life destroyed
Juana tries to throw the pearl back into the sea. Kino stops her and beats her up.
   He is attacked again, and this time he kills one of his enemies. Others, meanwhile, break his canoe and burn his house.

Chapter 6: Death and return
Kino and his family escape into the desert. Trackers are sent to hunt them, and Coyotito is killed.
   Kino and Juana return to their village and throw the pearl back into the sea.

Five movements

The presence of music in *The Pearl* suggests a symphonic structure in the plot. The story and thematic development can be studied in five musical movements or stages, with each stage corresponding to an appropriate physical setting and its own thematic mood.

1st movement: The beach (Chapter 1)
Man builds his own way of life and his civilisation on the beach, between sea and desert. This movement introduces the various thematic elements: man, nature, society, evil. It ends on a note of conflict that looks forward.

2nd movement: The sea (Chapter 2)
Microcosm of life, death, and procreation in nature. The pearl reflects the moral cycle of hope, illusion, despair, and reality.

3rd movement: The town (Chapters 3–5)
Conflict: the events which take place after Kino finds the pearl reflect the 'death' stage of the natural cycle; and the 'illusion and despair' stage of the moral cycle. Although not all these events take place in the town, the town reflects the world of repression and deceit which surround Kino and his family at this stage.

4th movement: The desert and the mountains (Chapter 6, pages 65–84)
Flight, suffering, and purification. From the cave in the mountain top, Kino and Juana get a vision or overall perspective of existence; the cave symbolises rebirth.

5th movement: The sea (Chapter 6, pages 84–6)
Return to the ordinary level of human experience. But Kino and Juana are set apart from life after their traumatic experience.
The pearl is returned to the sea (the natural cycle) to await another cycle of life, death, and rebirth; and hope, suffering, despair, and vision.

Characterisation

Methods of characterisation in *The Pearl* include:

(*i*) description and comment by the author
(*ii*) description and comment by one character about another character
(*iii*) revelation through action or behaviour
(*iv*) revelation through dialogue or speech

Kino

His appearance: young, strong, black hair, thin moustache, bright eyes (p.3).
His way of life: fisherman and pearl diver, wakes at dawn, eats monotonous food (p.4). His way of life is hard and simple.
His family: wife Juana, child Coyotito.
Has strong emotional nature: kills scorpion (p.5), smashes his fist on doctor's gate (p.12), howls upon discovery that Coyotito is well after he finds the pearl (p.20), feels rage and hatred for the doctor (p.29), strikes Juana (p.55), feels depressed (pp.52,72).
Has great courage: attacks the intruder (p.36), goes outside to find the enemy at night (p.53), wants to lead the trackers away from his family (p.74), attacks the hunter and trackers alone (pp.80–2); shows both courage and imagination (pp.24,56).
Kino's people: used to make songs (pp.1,16), have a secret method for preserving canoes (p.14), have been exploited by the more dominant race in Mexico (pp.9,29).

Juana

Simple appearance (p.3), believes in both Christianity and old Indian religion (pp.4,17), a good wife (p.7), can bear much physical pain and hardship (p.7), loves her son (p.7), has woman's qualities of reason, caution, and sense of preservation (p.56).

The doctor

From the beggars' view: avaricious, cruel, ignorant (p.9).
Way of life: luxurious but he is discontented (p.10).
After Kino finds the pearl, the doctor's greed is awakened: he poisons Coyotito in order to pretend to save his life and thus gain Kino's gratitude; he may be the intruder in Kino's house.

The pearl buyers

Really all are controlled by one man (p.40).
First pearl buyer is very cunning (p.45).

The attackers, trackers, hunter

Not identified: nameless because this makes them more terrifying, also more impersonal.
Described in terms of darkness and evil (pp.36–7,52,80).

The villagers (and townspeople)

Fill in the background.
Express Steinbeck's views indirectly; example: the beggars. Also perform a choric role, commenting on the central action; example: the different reactions to Kino's discovery of the pearl (pp.21,41), and later to his defiance of the pearl buyers (p.50).

The priest

Appears briefly (pp.21,26–7,43).
Not a good priest, as he does not tend to the needs of the poor in his parish. He also abuses religious teachings to keep the Indians down (p.43). Seems to be a greedy man, as he only visits Kino because he hopes Kino will give money to the church.

The setting

The sea

Basic image of life: rich sea bottom alive with growing things (p.13), becomes microcosm of moral universe also as pearl sinks back into sea (p.86).
The beach represents narrow strip of human civilisation (p.13) between the sea and the desert, both powerful natural forces that can become inhospitable to man, for instance, the Gulf storm (p.63).

The mountains

Described as monlithic, high bare stone (p.75), also refuge for fleeing animals and the family (p.73). The pools of water in the mountain (p.75) are places of life and also death (p.76).
The cave (pp.77–80) where the family hides becomes a place of death (perhaps sacrifice) for Coyotito (p.84); also suggests rebirth. Mountain, pools, and cave are the scene for climax of the novella.

The town

Compared to a colonial animal (p.21) because its organisation is like an organic system in an animal.
Is situated on the narrow strip of beach and estuary between sea and mountain (p.13).
Description of town is typical of Spanish-Mexican city (p.8).

The Gulf

The Gulf air is uncertain; has a mirage-like effect, so that people cannot always believe or trust what they see (pp.13–14). This ambiguous effect influences all of life in La Paz: even the pearl seems to be deceptive.

The style

Combination of styles

(*1*) *Realistic and impressionistic description*

SCENERY: outside Kino's house (pp.1–2)
the desert (pp.66,72–3)
the mountains (p.75)

BUILDINGS: interior of Kino's house (pp.2–4)
the town (p.8)
the doctor's chamber (p.10)
the pearl buyers' offices (p.44)

PHYSICAL ACTION: Kino climbing down from the cave (pp.80–1)

FACTUAL INFORMATION: how pearls are formed (pp.15–16)

CHARACTER PORTRAITS: the doctor (p.10)
the first pearl buyer (pp.44–5)

(*2*) *Dramatic dialogue*

In many scenes, dialogue is used to reveal character, or to develop a theme. The most effective dialogue is used in the following places: the doctor visits Kino and asks about the pearl (p.34); the conversation between Kino and his brother (pp.51,61–4); and the bargaining for the pearl (pp.45–50). Dialogue is usually used together with ordinary narrative.

(*3*) *Narrative style*

Steinbeck's normal narrative style in *The Pearl* is a simple, unpretentious style that reflects the simplicity of the villagers. This style is appropriate, for Steinbeck wanted *The Pearl* to have the feeling of a retold tale, a folk-tale told over many generations by uncomplicated villagers. His narrative style makes story-telling smooth.

(*4*) *Poetic style*

In crucial places of the novel, the style becomes very highly charged with emotional and symbolic content. This style can be seen particularly in the description of the pearl (p.19), and the Gulf mirage (pp.13–14). Two main stylistic techniques enhance the poetic quality of the style in *The Pearl*: the songs and the imagery.

THE SONGS: increase the emotional intensity of major episodes; add a musical dimension.

IMAGERY: of light, shadow, darkness, night.

Cinematic technique

The novella is influenced by cinematic technique, particularly in its visual brilliancy, the use of thematic music and background (animal) noises, and the use of light imagery. The brooding sense of the Gulf mirage also conveys an overall mood or atmosphere upon the whole novella.

A parable

The main features in *The Pearl* which make it a parable, or 'retold' tale, include:

THE FRAMEWORK: Steinbeck's introduction to the story, and the first paragraph of the conclusion (p.84);

THE SIMPLE NARRATIVE STYLE: the story resembles a tale handed down through the generations;

THE SIMPLIFIED CHARACTERISATION: Kino represents Man, and Juana represents Woman;

THE MORAL MEANING: it is possible to draw a hidden moral meaning from the novella.

The arrangement of material

In order to answer examination questions fully and effectively, you should arrange your material so that it forms a cohesive answer, and proves the thesis or point of your argument. Try as far as possible to have one main idea which controls the whole argument. Sometimes it may be difficult to find the main idea, if the question is vague or rather general. In this case, try to pin-point the relevance of the topic to the text.

To begin with, you should establish what aspect of the text the question is concerned with: theme, character, general background, setting, ideas, structure, imagery, and so on. Sometimes the arrangement of your answer will follow naturally once you have decided what aspect of the novella the question deals with.

(1) Questions about theme may be approached from many different angles, depending on the nature of the question. Whatever method, or combination of methods, you use, it is doubtful whether your answer would be complete unless it also incorporated analysis. Try to avoid merely describing or narrating something (scene, character, image, and so on): evaluate the significance of what you are saying. For example, if you describe the first pearl buyer's coin trick, you should also point out that the trick reveals the deceitful and cunning aspect of his character.

Descriptive approach
Select the main features of the subject to be described. Formulate any developments which have changed the subject.

EXAMPLE: Discuss the physical background of *The Pearl*.

State the main physical locations of the narrative: sea, beach, village, town, desert, mountain, and cave. It is apparent that a purely descriptive approach is unsatisfactory: we need to evaluate the significance of each physical region (unless the question expressly asks for description only).

Organisation of this sort of answer is nevertheless fairly straightforward: taking each of the regions given above in turn, discuss its significance to the theme.

Historical and sociological approach
Trace the past history of the subject under discussion, followed by an analysis of the present condition of things.

EXAMPLE: Describe the way of life of the Gulf Indians.

Describe the past history of the Gulf Indians: mention the two major traditions of their culture, the songs and the canoes; describe the effects of Spanish rule, including the doctor's attitude towards the Indians, and Kino's confused reaction to the doctor.

Describe how the Indians live now: the fishing village, including Kino's house, can be described; also the way they look for pearls. Do not forget to stress the warmth of the sense of community among the Indians.

Describe the Indians' religious beliefs: a mixture of Christianity and their old religion, to show how old traditions still grip them firmly.

Briefly compare the Indians' existence with the town way of life: describe the difference in the buildings, the doctor's food and clothing.

Discuss Kino's failure to get a fair price for the pearl: analyse Juan Tomás's warning, and the significance of the priest's sermon. This can be your conclusion: an evaluation of how hard it is for the Gulf Indians to change their way of life.

Narrative approach

Organise your material according to the major events of the plot; or the five days of the story; or (if the question deals with a section of the book only) the stages of the episode concerned.

EXAMPLE: What is the effect of the pearl on Kino?

Give an introductory sketch of Kino's character and way of life before he finds the pearl. Mention his family life; also the emotional tension he feels which is brought out by the visit to the doctor.

Then trace the stages of change in Kino, brought about by finding the pearl: first, delight and hope; second, fear and loneliness; third, violence, suspicion, and cunning; fourth, the complete destruction of the old way of life; fifth, the animal-like qualities of flight, including his bravery; sixth, the final state of removal from ordinary life.

Kino's development can also be compared with Juana's transformation, or even the changes in the people as a whole. The question may require such a comparison; also, a comparison adds depth to your answer.

Moral approach

Discuss the ethical aspects of the subject. You will probably need to refer to background material, such as the novella's idea of luck, the gods, the idea of good and evil, the idea of humanity, and so on. You could, in fact, organise your material so that you discuss each of these ideas in turn; at the same time tracing the relationships between them.

EXAMPLE: Discuss the symbolism of the pearl.

Describe the pearl's discovery and appearance, making clear why these two points suggest that the pearl is symbolic.

State the symbolism of the pearl: what does it symbolise? Discuss the dream forms, the desires it arouses in people. Is the pearl good, or is it evil? Does the novella tell us this?

Discuss the changes in the pearl. When and why do these changes occur? What do they reflect? Relate the changes to changes in people.

What is the nature of the evil associated with the pearl? Why is it impersonal? Discuss the idea of fate (luck or chance) as this is conceived by Kino and Juana. Why does Coyotito die?

You may conclude with analysing the return of Kino and Juana. Why do they throw the pearl back into the sea? What is the pearl's appearance as it falls into the sea? What happens to the pearl in the sea bottom? Why?

In organising your material, you may have discovered that not one, but many, approaches to the subject may be involved. Just remember to state the main argument as clearly as possible.

(2) Questions about characterisation may require a description of the character; an evaluation of the character's function in the novella, and the techniques used to portray the character; and an analysis of how the character relates to other aspects of theme and meaning.

Character portraits

These are straightforward questions. You need to remember, however, that a mere list of the character's attributes will make a poor answer: disorganised, and unfocused. Start with the character's basic qualities, and use additional information to illustrate these qualities, or to modify them. Often, in order to give a comprehensive picture, it is necessary to see the character in terms of the theme.

EXAMPLE: Describe the character of the doctor.

Give a brief account of the doctor's moral nature. Refer to the view of the beggars: is this a useful summary?

Analyse the scene of the doctor in his chamber: use the physical details to support your moral judgements.

Give the history of the conflict between the Indians and the doctor's race. Use Kino's reaction as an illustration. Mention the view of the fishermen.

Analyse the doctor's behaviour after Kino finds the pearl. What new information about him does this show?

Briefly conclude with an estimation of how successful the characterisation is.

Character plus theme or technique

Such questions involve an understanding of how the character relates to certain ideas or themes, and of what novelistic techniques have been used to build up the meaning.

EXAMPLE: Describe the character of Juana in relation to the theme.

Describe Juana's character in the beginning (make use of material in Chapter 1), pointing out her appearance, her moral characteristics, and her roles as wife and mother. Remember her beliefs too.

How far does Juana's character reflect the novella's differentiation between man and woman (p.56)?

Show what aspects of Juana's character are brought out in each of the following stages: discovery of the pearl; after each attack on Kino; discovery of the dead man; in the desert; and upon her return to La Paz. These stages also reflect the development of the theme, so you are analysing both her character and the theme together.

(3) Questions on technique are generally related to various aspects of theme or characterisation. For instance, the question, 'Discuss the sym-

bolism of the pearl' (given above) is also a question about technique. For some questions on technique, you may need to go into various aspects of a certain technique: discuss them in turn, but formulate an overall evaluation of how successfully such a technique has been used. An example appears below.

EXAMPLE: Discuss the influence of cinematic technique on *The Pearl*.

Describe the background to Steinbeck's writing on *The Pearl*, briefly, and as far as this relates to cinematic technique: his interest in film, his own film scripts, the Mexican films, the fact that *The Pearl* was also filmed.

Analyse the main features of cinematic influence on *The Pearl*: visual detail and clarity; background and thematic music, and sound effects; use of lighting effects.

Conclude briefly with an evaluation of how effective such techniques are in the novella.

(4) Concluding remarks: some general principles to bear in mind when preparing an answer are given below.

Collect all the relevant, significant information on the topic, including any quotations you can use.

Analyse the information: is there a common idea or theme running through your data? Is there any consecutive development of a theme or idea or character, and so on? Are there key words or phrases which occur in a developing pattern?

Organise the information, according to the main ideas that the information reveals. Usually, when you approach a question, you should have formed some conclusions about the novella already. Use these conclusions as the organising ideas.

Begin and end your argument decisively.

The list of quotations below has also been arranged in such a way as to suggest possible methods of arranging material for your answers.

Useful quotations

This is a list of quotations, which may be useful in answering questions on the text. The list is divided into groups, with each group of quotations illustrating a major aspect of the novella. Some brief notes are included to help you understand the quotations.

This list is not, of course, exhaustive. There will be other quotations that are perhaps more relevant to the question you wish to answer. Try to make a list of your own to supplement this one.

The Pearl

(1) Finding the pearl

'But the pearls were accidents, and the finding of one was luck, a little pat on the back by God or the gods or both' (p.16).

'Chance was against it, but luck and the gods might be for it . . . Juana was making the magic of prayer . . . to tear the luck out of the gods' hands' (p.17).

'It is not good to want a thing too much. It sometimes drives the luck away. You must want it just enough, and you must be very tactful with God or the gods' (p.19).

The Indian view of the Christian God is heavily influenced by the old Indian religion (the gods). Thus Juana thinks that they must almost force the gods to help them, although this must be done with care as the gods do not like human demands. There is also the sense that luck (chance, coincidence, good fortune) governs life.

(2) Its appearance

'Kino lifted the flesh, and there it lay, the great pearl, perfect as the moon. It captured the light and refined it and gave it back in silver incandescence. It was as large as a seagull's egg. It was the greatest pearl in the world . . . In the surface of the great pearl he could see dream forms. He picked the pearl from the dying flesh and held it in his palm' (p.19).

'And the beauty of the pearl, winking and glimmering in the light of the little candle, cozened his brain with its beauty . . . its music of promise and delight, its guarantee of the future, of comfort, of security' (p.38).

The beauty of the pearl is mixed with many other qualities, which are hidden at this point but which will emerge later. The pearl evokes 'dream forms' that become both illusion and nightmare. Harsh reality is hinted at through the 'dying flesh' of the pearl, and the hurt hand of Kino.

(3) Evilness of the pearl

'"This thing is evil," she cried harshly. "This pearl is like a sin! It will destroy us"' (p.37).

'"This pearl is evil . . . Kino, it is evil, it is evil!"' (p.54).

Juana recognises the dangerous illusion of hope in the pearl. Her words of warning mark each stage of the crisis, after each battle with the intruders of the night.

'And Kino thrust the pearl back into his clothing, and the music of the pearl had become sinister in his ears, and it was interwoven with the music of evil' (p.68).

In the desert, Kino finally recognises the evil brought by the pearl, when he sees the horrible images of dying in the pearl, and hears its distorted music.

'And the pearl was ugly; it was grey, like a malignant growth. And Kino heard the music of the pearl, distorted and insane' (p.86).

In the end, the lovely pearl has become ugly: the initial hope has become total disillusionment. Thus the pearl's appearance actually reflects the spiritual condition of man.

The plot

The quotations in this group illustrate major crises in the plot.

(1) Kino's broken hand

'Then, without warning, he struck the gate a crushing blow with his fist. He looked down in wonder . . . at the blood that flowed down between his fingers' (p.12).

Kino's angry reaction here catches up many aspects of *The Pearl*. The crushed hand is a recurrent image which reminds us of the deep-seated hatred in him. Each time he holds the pearl in his right hand, it is a reminder of the real and harsh world he lives in (see p.28). It is also an image of the conflict between Kino's people and the doctor's people (the Indian-Mexicans and the Spanish-Mexicans).

(2) Juan Tomás's warning

'"You have defied not the pearl buyers, but the whole structure, the whole way of life"' (p.51). These words indicate the meaning of Kino's defiance. By refusing to sell the pearl, he has upset the whole system. Juan Tomás further warns him against too high expectations elsewhere: '"But I wonder if you will find it any different in the capital"' (p.51), suggesting that life is the same everywhere. Kino's action has made people think about the whole system: '"If that is so, then all of us have been cheated all of our lives"' (p.50).

(3) The past is destroyed

'This was an evil beyond thinking. The killing of a man was not so evil as the killing of a boat. . . . There was sorrow in Kino's rage, but this last thing had tightened him beyond breaking. He was an animal now . . . and he lived only to preserve himself and his family' (p.59).

'All of the time Juana had been trying to rescue something of the old peace, of the time before the pearl. But now it was gone, and there was no retrieving it. And knowing this, she abandoned the past instantly. There was nothing to do but to save themselves' (p.57).

It is the body of the dead man in the path which convinces Juana of the necessity of flight. This marks the midway point in their lives, for they can never turn back now (see also Juana's words on page 72). Juana's realisation here is subtly different from Kino's thoughts about the change in their lives: 'But Kino had lost his old world and he must clamber on to a new one' (p.51); 'he had broken through the horizons into a cold and lonely outside. He felt alone and unprotected' (p.27).

The situation is more desperate now: they really have lost their choice of going back to the old way of life. The destruction of the canoe and Kino's house thus symbolises the destruction of the old peaceful way of life; and the destruction of the civilised (or social) aspect of man's nature, so that Kino and Juana must rely on primitive instinct to stay alive.

(4) The return

'The people say that the two seemed to be removed from human experience; that they had gone through pain and had come out on the other side; that there was almost a magical protection about them' (p.85).

The return of Kino and Juana is seen through the eyes of people remembering the event (see p.84), setting the event into the framework of the 'parable' once more. Kino and Juana are characterised by a strange distancing from ordinary life, which suggests that the experience they have been through has a profoundly spiritual meaning.

The characters

(1) Kino and Juana

'He had said: "I am a man," and that meant certain things to Juana. It meant that he was half insane and half god. It meant that Kino would drive his strength against a mountain and plunge his strength against the sea ... Sometimes the quality of woman, the reason, the caution, the sense of preservation, could cut through Kino's manness and save them all' (p.56).

'Kino was young and strong ... His eyes were warm and fierce and bright' (p.3).

'Kino had wondered often at the iron in his patient, fragile wife. She, who was obedient and respectful and cheerful and patient, could bear physical pain with hardly a cry' (p.7).

'Every year Kino refinished his canoe with the hard shell-like plaster by the secret method that had also come to him from his father. Now he came to the canoe and touched the bow tenderly as he always did' (p.14).

'It was very good—Kino closed his eyes again to listen to his music. Perhaps he alone did this and perhaps all of his people did it' (p.1).

Kino and Juana live a simple, traditional life, hard but uncorrupted by modern civilisation. Their strength (both physical and spiritual) derives from this fact.

(2) The doctor

'The doctor never came to the cluster of brush houses' (p.7).

The beggars 'knew the doctor. They knew his ignorance, his cruelty, his avarice, his appetites, his sins. They knew his clumsy operations and the little brown pennies he gave sparingly for alms' (p.9).

'This doctor was of a race which for nearly four hundred years had beaten and starved and robbed and despised Kino's race, and frightened it too' (p.9).

'His eyes rested in puffy little hammocks of flesh and his mouth drooped with discontent' (p.10).

The character of the doctor is given explicitly by Steinbeck. His actions after Kino's discovery of the pearl merely illustrate the facts given above.

(3) The pearl buyers

'Now there was only one pearl buyer with many hands' (p.40).

'Although these men would not profit beyond their salaries, there was excitement among the pearl buyers, for there was excitement in the hunt' (p.40).

Images of nature

(1) The pool of life

'The sea bottom was rich with crawling and swimming and growing things' (p.13).

'Out in the estuary a tight woven school of small fishes . . . broke water to escape a school of great fishes that drove in to eat them. And in the houses the people could hear . . . as the slaughter went on' (p.32).

'The little pools were places of life because of the water, and places of killing because of the water, too' (p.76).

The different water pools (sea bottom, estuary, and mountain pool) are a microcosm of the universe as a whole. They also reflect the processes of living, dying, and procreating as natural aspects of the cycle of existence.

(2) *The Gulf mirage*

'The hazy mirage was up. The uncertain air . . . hung over the whole Gulf so that all sights were unreal and vision could not be trusted . . . Thus it might be that the people of the Gulf trust things of the spirit and things of the imagination' (pp.13–14).

The strange, ambiguous atmosphere of the Gulf seems to affect all of life. The pearl, too, is part of this vague, deceptive world.

(3) *The ants*

'Kino watched with the detachment of God while a dusty ant frantically tried to escape the sand trap an ant lion had dug for him' (p.2).

'He watched the ants moving . . . and he put his foot in their path. Then [they] climbed over his instep and continued on [their] way, and Kino left his foot there and watched them move over it' (p.67).

This image of Kino and the ants suggests an analogy with human beings and 'God' or 'the gods'. The gods seem to be indifferent to man's actions, although they may be able to exert an influence upon man's life. However, there seems to be a natural force which drives man onward towards his destiny, for the ants continue on the way despite the presence of Kino's foot.

Context questions

Read the following passages and then answer the questions which follow:

Passage A

Kino stared into the dimness of the little office, for his eyes were squeezed from the outside glare. But the buyer's eyes had become as steady and cruel and unwinking as a hawk's eyes, while the rest of his face smiled in greeting. And secretly, behind his desk, his right hand practised with the coin.

'I have a pearl,' said Kino. And Juan Tomás stood beside him and snorted a little at the understatement. The neighbours peered around the doorway, and a line of little boys clambered on the window bars and looked through (p.45).

(1) What is the meaning of 'understatement' in this context?
(2) What is the thematic significance of the contrast between the brightness outside and the dimness inside the office?
(3) What aspect of the buyer's character is shown here?
(4) What is the buyer doing with the coin, and what does this reveal about him?
(5) Why are the neighbours looking into the office?

Passage B

The neighbours, close pressed and silent in the house, nodded their heads at his wild imaginings. And a man in the rear murmured: 'A rifle. He will have a rifle.'

But the music of the pearl was shrilling with triumph in Kino. Juana looked up, and her eyes were wide at Kino's courage and at his imagination. And electric strength had come to him now the horizons were kicked out (pp.24–5).

(1) Explain the meaning of: 'the horizons were kicked out'.
(2) Why are the neighbours so impressed by Kino?
(3) Why is it ironic for Kino to desire a rifle?
(4) What difference between Kino and Juana is implied in this passage?
(5) Why does Steinbeck suggest that Kino grows stronger now?

Passage C

And then from above came a little murmuring cry. The watcher turned his head to listen and then he stood up, and one of the sleepers stirred on the ground and awakened and asked quietly: 'What is it?'

'I don't know,' said the watcher. 'It sounded like a cry, almost like a human—like a baby.'

The man who had been sleeping said: 'You can't tell. Some coyote bitch with a litter. I've heard a coyote pup cry like a baby.'

The sweat rolled in drops down Kino's forehead and fell into his eyes and burned them (p.82).

(1) What, probably, do the words 'from above' indicate?
(2) Who are the watcher and the sleepers?
(3) What is the significance of a coyote in this context?
(4) What is Kino doing?
(5) Where is the conversation taking place? Describe the scene briefly.

Interpretative questions

The questions below are arranged in increasing order of difficulty. This section of the Notes ends with model answers.

(1) What is the main theme of the novel?

(2) What are the major features of Steinbeck's realistic style in *The Pearl*?

(3) Describe the sociological background of *The Pearl*.

(4) Steinbeck differentiates between man and woman (p.56). To what extent does his characterisation of Kino and Juana reflect such a difference?

(5) Relate the development of Kino's character to the theme.

(6) Steinbeck states in his introduction to *The Pearl* that 'perhaps everyone takes his own meaning from it and reads his own life into it'. What possible interpretations can you make of the novella?

(7) *The Pearl* has been described as 'a morality set to music': to what degree is this a useful description?

(8) How far is it true that the uncertain Gulf air distorts reality in *The Pearl*?

(9) Why does Steinbeck refuse to identify Kino's attackers and hunters? Relate your answer to the moral background of the book.

Model answers

How does Steinbeck differentiate between man and woman in
The Pearl? How significant is this difference?

Steinbeck's concept of the difference between man and woman is traditional rather than modern. He assigns definite and separate roles and functions to men and women. It would be quite fair to say that all the characters in the novel play traditional roles, in the sense that they are revealed only in one aspect. They are what is known as flat, or undeveloped, characters. Thus, the priest is only a (bad) priest: he is not shown in any other capacity. Steinbeck is drawing a picture of a traditional community, with its priest, doctor, merchants, fishermen, pearl divers, and even beggars; and no one succeeds in disrupting this traditional stability. On the whole, people do not question the validity of their traditional society. Their protest, when voiced, is raised against social exploitation, rather than against their inherent roles.

The differentiation between masculine and feminine roles tends to support such a view of the community in *The Pearl*. Most of the characters are men, the only women being Juana, Apolonia (the wife of Juan Tomas), the doctor's mistress, and the very minor and unnamed women of the town. The minor figures are easily characterised. The 'hard-faced' mistress is barely mentioned; the women in town are just 'mothers'; Apolonia is seen only in the role of the grief-stricken sister-in-law. All these figures have one-dimensional functions and are not fleshed out as people.

In the same way, the minor male characters perform only their conventional roles: as priest, doctor, merchant, beggar, fisherman, or servant.

The two main characters, Kino and Juana, are the only ones who are conscious of a struggle to transform their conventional social functions, aided to some degree by Kino's brother Juan Tomas. They are not revolutionaries against the traditional designation of male and female roles, although Juan Tomás warns Kino that what he is attempting to do threatens the whole way of life of their world. Kino, as an individual, defies the economic and social structure of his society, when he refuses to sell the pearl in La Paz; and Kino has the complete support of his wife although she too warns him about his great daring. The significant thing, however, is that Kino leads in this revolution, and Juana follows. She pleads with him to change his mind, she admonishes him for exposing his whole family to danger, but in the end she agrees with him and lends her strength to what he is doing; partly because she, too, believes in their great endeavour, but mainly because she trusts Kino as a man.

In Juana's mind, being a man signified a very definite thing. When Kino had said in explanation of his actions, 'I am a man', that meant to Juana that 'he was half insane and half god'. Man was godlike in that he would not accept defeat without a struggle. He was willing (or was driven) to pitch his strength against insurmountable odds, although the attempt might destroy him. This almost insane drive in him was what differentiated him from a woman.

Juana, as a woman, could not really understand the nature of Kino's determination to fight against the whole structure of life in their world, but she could accept such a quality. As a woman, Juana complemented her husband and, with him, she felt whole and complete. Woman, as Steinbeck explains, represented the qualities of reason, caution, and the sense of preservation, while man was courage and imagination. The two were dependent on each other.

At its conclusion, *The Pearl* confirms this view of man and woman. Kino offers the pearl to Juana, but she declines it, and it is he who finally throws it back into the sea. However, something rather surprising has taken place before this event. As Kino and Juana enter La Paz, the people notice that they are not walking in single file with Kino ahead and Juana following, as is customary, but side by side. It is as though their terrible experience has removed them from the plane of ordinary existence. In the realm of their unique tragedy, they have become equal, sharing a common vision into the meaning of life, which is normally denied to man.

Describe the village and town societies in the novella

The Pearl presents two facets of a Mexican society on the Gulf: an Indian-Mexican fishing village which huddles on the beach and a Spanish-Mexican town which rises on the fringes of the village. Village and town have distinct features of their own, but they form an integral and unified whole, which Steinbeck compares to 'a colonial animal'.

The village comprises a 'cluster of brush houses', whose simple appearance reflects the lives of the Indians living there. The bareness of the interior of Kino's house is typical: dirt floor, walls with chinks that let in the weather, a fire hole, sleeping mats, and a box for Coyotito. At night, Kino can hear the whispering of his neighbours, for the Indians do not sleep through the night, and the houses are close together. The communal sense is strong in the village. Events in Kino's family are not just personal to them, but affect the whole community. Neighbours come rushing to see and to sympathise when Coyotito is stung by a scorpion; they accompany Juana to the doctor's house; and everyone is involved with the selling of the pearl. Perhaps the deepest evidence of the wholeness of the village can be felt in Kino's integrity after his canoe is broken. He refuses to retaliate or to steal one of his neighbours' canoes in return, although he desperately needs a canoe to take his family to safety.

The canoes represent the ancient past of Kino's people and thus are more than monetary objects. They form a link with the richness of the past, which has been obliterated by the Spanish conquest. Only the canoes and the songs remain.

The more dominant society of the Spanish-Mexicans is centred on the town. In appearance, the town, too, is typical of its kind: outer walls that mark the junction between the brush houses and the stone and plaster buildings inside. The doctor's house, with its cool inner gardens, and 'caged birds' singing poignantly, and the smell of rich food, contrasts sharply with Kino's tumbledown house and spare, monotonous diet.

The physical contrasts between town and village are symbolic of the submerged antagonisms between the Indians and the Spanish-Mexicans. Like the doctor, the Spanish-Mexicans are on the whole materially better off. The wealth of the town is controlled by them, particularly the pearl trade, which is, in fact, in the hands of one man only. Thus an effective monopoly exists, which ensures that the Indians cannot upset the existing state of things. The Spanish religion, too, has been utilised to ensure compliance from the Indians.

The conflict between village and town, between Indian and Spanish-Mexican, has its origins in history. Steinbeck formulates a long tradition of exploitation of the Gulf Indians by a conquering race, which 'had beaten and starved and robbed and despised Kino's race' for four centuries.

Consequently, the fear, rage, and hatred felt by the Indians are buried deep, as Kino's confused reaction to the doctor shows. His subsequent defiance of the pearl buyers is thus not just a refusal to sell his pearl. It is a challenge to the whole structure of society in La Paz, as Juan Tomás warns him. Kino has threatened the 'whole way of life' and Juan Tomás hints that he may never escape, for the same system probably exists everywhere. He suggests to Kino that the Gulf Indians have always managed to 'survive'. His words may reflect a deeper understanding of the nature of life.

Though there are sharp antagonisms between Indians and Spanish-Mexicans in La Paz, nevertheless, the town as a whole is still 'a colonial animal'. Its existence is characterised by an interdependency of all things within it. The parts depend on each other, affect each other, and the whole is finally something different from the sum of the parts. Juan Tomás's words, in fact, point to the idea of the wholeness of life, which the old Indian religion enunciated, and which forms a philosophical basis to the novella.

Part 5

Suggestions for further reading

The text

STEINBECK, JOHN: *The Pearl*, Heinemann Educational Books (New Windmill Series), London, 1977. This is a reliable edition, although others are available: they are listed in A note on the text, p.13.

Other works by the author

STEINBECK, JOHN: *The Log from the Sea of Cortez*, Pan Books, London, 1969. This contains the original story for *The Pearl*, some information about the Gulf of Mexico, and a discussion of non-teleological philosophy.

STEINBECK, JOHN: *Tortilla Flat*, The Modern Library, New York, 1937. Its view of Spanish, Indian, and Mexican Americans forms an interesting contrast to *The Pearl*.

STEINBECK, JOHN: *The Grapes of Wrath*, Viking Press, New York, 1972. Text and criticism edited by Peter Lisca. Steinbeck's most well-known novel.

General reading

DAVIS, ROBERT MURRAY (ED.): *Steinbeck: A Collection of Critical Essays*, Prentice-Hall, Englewood Cliffs, New Jersey, 1972. Contains a discussion of the uneasy mixture of realism with allegory in *The Pearl*.

FONTENROSE, JOSEPH: *John Steinbeck: An Introduction and Interpretation*, Holt Rinehart and Winston, New York, 1963. Contains an interpretation of *The Pearl* as 'a morality set to music'.

FRENCH, WARREN: *John Steinbeck*, College and University Press, New Haven, 1961. An analysis of why *The Pearl* is a 'defective' book.

HAYASHI, TETSUMARO (ED.): *A Study Guide to Steinbeck: A Handbook to his Major Works*, The Scarecrow Press, Inc., Metuchen, N.J., 1974. Includes a guide to *The Pearl*, containing background information, plot synopsis, critical explication, suggestions for research, and selected bibliography. Also has a critique of the filmed version of *The Pearl*.

KIERNAN, THOMAS: *The Intricate Music: A Biography of Steinbeck*, Little, Brown, New York, 1979. First full-length treatment of Steinbeck's life, although not the definitive biography.

LISCA, PETER: *The Wide World of John Steinbeck*, Rutgers University Press, New Brunswick, 1958. Pays particular attention to the blending of 'the realistic and the lyric' style of *The Pearl*.

WATT, F.W.: *John Steinbeck*, Oliver and Boyd, Edinburgh, 1962; Grove Press, New York, 1962. A good general introduction to Steinbeck. Discusses *The Pearl* briefly as part of Steinbeck's criticism of American civilisation.

The author of these notes

MARGARET YONG was educated in England and at the Universities of Singapore and Malaya. She worked as an English teacher in a secondary school, and then taught English as a Second Language in the University of Malaya, before joining its English Department. She has published articles in *Pacific Quarterly* (NZ) and *Dewan Sastra* (Malysia) and is currently working on New Literatures in English for her Ph.D. She is writing an article on women playwrights for the University of Malaya's project on the role of women in Malaysia.

YORK HANDBOOKS

The first ten titles

YORK HANDBOOKS form a companion series to York Notes and are designed to meet the wider needs of students of English and related fields. Each volume is a compact study of a given subject area, written by an authority with experience in communicating the essential ideas to students of all levels.

AN INTRODUCTORY GUIDE TO ENGLISH LITERATURE
by MARTIN STEPHEN

PREPARING FOR EXAMINATIONS IN ENGLISH LITERATURE
by NEIL McEWAN

AN INTRODUCTION TO LITERARY CRITICISM
by RICHARD DUTTON

THE ENGLISH NOVEL
by IAN MILLIGAN

ENGLISH POETRY
by CLIVE T. PROBYN

STUDYING CHAUCER
by ELISABETH BREWER

STUDYING SHAKESPEARE
by MARTIN STEPHEN *and* PHILIP FRANKS

ENGLISH USAGE
by COLIN G. HEY

A DICTIONARY OF LITERARY TERMS
by MARTIN GRAY

READING THE SCREEN
An Introduction to Film Studies
by JOHN IZOD